24769 Dewdney Trunk Road
Maple Ridge, B.C. V4R 1X2

Extraordinary Jobs in the

SERVICE SECTOR

Also in the Extraordinary Jobs series:

Extraordinary Jobs in the

SERVICE SECTOR

ALECIA T. DEVANTIER & CAROL A. TURKINGTON

Ferguson
An imprint of Infobase Publishing

Ferguson
An imprint of Infobase Publishing
132 West 31st Street
New York NY 10001

Devantier, Alecia T.
  Extraordinary jobs in the service sector / Alecia T. Devantier and Carol A. Turkington.
    p. cm.—(Extraordinary jobs series)
  Includes bibliographical references and index.
  ISBN 0-8160-5863-6 (hc: alk. paper)
1. Service industries—United States—Juvenile literature. 2. Service industries—Juvenile literature. I. Turkington, Carol. II. Title.
  HD9981.5.D48 2007
  331.702—dc 22   2006017910

Ferguson books are available at special discounts when purchased in bulk quantities for businesses, associations, institutions, or sales promotions. Please call our Special Sales Department in New York at (212) 967-8800 or (800) 322-8755.

You can find Ferguson on the World Wide Web at http://www.fergpubco.com

Text design by Mary Susan Ryan-Flynn
Cover design Salvatore Luongo

Printed in the United States of America

VB MSRF 10 9 8 7 6 5 4 3 2 1

This book is printed on acid-free paper.

CONTENTS

ACKNOWLEDGMENTS

This book wouldn't have been possible without the help of countless others who referred us to individuals to interview and came up with information about a wide variety of odd and unusual jobs. We deeply appreciate the time and generosity of all those individuals who took the time to talk to us about their unusual jobs in the service sector. Thanks also to all the people who helped with interviews and information and the production of this book. Thanks also to our editors James Chambers and Sarah Fogarty, to Vanessa Nittoli, to our agents Ed Claflin of Ed Claflin Literary Associates and Gene Brissie of James Peter Associates, and to Michael and Kara.

ARE YOU CUT OUT FOR A CAREER SERVING OTHERS?

Your boss just told you that a bigger company has bought your firm, and they're not sure if there's a spot for you in the Big Picture. You've spent all your time slaving away at your job, staying late and coming in early, but now the company doesn't seem to be there for you.

At that point, it may occur to you that perhaps there's something more for you out there in the world of work than you've discovered so far. Perhaps there's a job where you can help others—people who will truly appreciate what you're doing for them. If you can't stand the thought of sitting at a desk every day, gazing out your window at the world passing you by, if you feel as if you're just not appreciated, then maybe you should consider a career serving others—whether it's working as a governess, serving as a butler, interpreting for deaf and hard-of-hearing clients, or transcribing written language into braille—think about some of these options. Let's face it: Some people just aren't cut out for a typical career path. But how do you know if you're more the governess, piano tuner, or concierge kind of person? Take some time to think about the kind of person you are and the sorts of experiences you dream of having.

First of all, ask yourself: *What am I passionate about?* Do you spend every waking moment thinking and dreaming about helping others? Do you think about teaching kids, advising hotel visitors of the latest exhibitions, or training beauty pageant contestants? Do you love the idea of taking care of someone else's estate, handling three or four or five huge homes all over the world and making sure everything ticks like clockwork? Does helping others seem like the very best kind of work there is?

If you follow your heart, you're almost guaranteed to find a career you love. In fact, almost every individual we interviewed for this book repeated the same litany—*I love my job. I love the independence. I love helping others.*

Many of these careers don't offer monetary rewards, yet to the people who pursue those careers, it doesn't seem to matter. What these jobs do offer is something much harder to measure—and that's a job that lets you do what you love to do and help others at the same time.

Of course, loving what you do is only part of having a successful career serving others. You also have to be good at what you want to do. Most jobs in which you serve others are so specialized that if you're going to go after one of them, you need to be really good at it. Whether you're thinking of becoming a nanny or wedding planner, you need to have the talent and the training to do that job better than most other people.

If you're like most of us, you've inherited a bevy of *shoulds* about the kind of person you are. These *shoulds* inside your head can be a major stumbling block in finding and enjoying a leisure career. Maybe other people won't be so happy with your career choice either. You may hear complaints from your family and friends who just can't understand why you don't want a "regular job." If you confide your career dreams to some of these people, they may try to discourage you. Can you handle their continuous skepticism, or downright disappointment? Other people often have their own *shoulds* for you too.

Or maybe you're having a hard time imagining a different path for yourself because of the obstacles you see. Maybe you're saying to yourself: "There's just no way I can follow my dream and make a living. I don't have the right education," or "I'm the wrong sex," or "I'm the wrong color." If you get bogged down in the belief that you can't follow your dream because of what is, you take away your power to discover what could be. You lose the power to create a different future.

A few people we've talked to in this book have always known exactly what they wanted to do, but almost everyone ended up with a job in the service industry by a circuitous route. It can take years to work up the courage to actually do what we knew all along we would have loved to do. You'll find that going after a job in the service industry is usually built slowly out of a variety of different experiences.

You don't have to start big. Try unique educational experiences—take a piano tuning class. Try an internship or unconventional job, a summer job, travel, or volunteer work.

Try not to think of learning and working as two totally separate things. When somebody hands you a diploma, you don't stop learning. School can be the best place to build up your fact-based knowledge; the rest of your life provides you with experience-based knowledge. You need both of those types of knowledge to forge a career in the service industry. Remember that this type of career is usually an active experience—take charge of your journey instead of relying on someone else's career path. Take advantage of the things you learn as you plan your next experience.

If you do decide to seek out a career in the service industry, you'll almost certainly encounter setbacks. How do you handle adversity? How do you feel when you fail? If you've always wanted to be an innsitter, how are you going to feel if you can't seem to break into the business, or no one wants to hire you? If you can pick yourself up and keep going, you've probably got the temperament to survive.

Going after the career you want means you'll need to look at the world through curious eyes—to wonder what's on the other side of the mountain and actually go there to find out. By exploring your options, you'll learn that work and play become the same thing. Push past your doubts and fears—and let your journey begin!

Carol A. Turkington
Alecia T. Devantier

HOW TO USE THIS BOOK

Students face a lot of pressure to decide what they want to be when they grow up. Some kids have discovered their passion right from the beginning: Some just love to work outdoors, while others are fascinated with science, mathematics, or languages. But what about those kids who just love to work in a job to benefit the other guy? Where can you go to learn about these exciting, service-oriented, nontraditional jobs?

For example, where can you go to find out how to become a cosmetologist for a funeral home? What does it take to become a governess or a nanny? Is it really possible to make a living as a matchmaker?

Look no further. This book will take you inside the world of a number of different service jobs, answering all sorts of questions you might have, letting you know what to expect if you pursue that career, introducing you to someone making a living that way, and providing resources if you want to do further research.

THE JOB PROFILES

All job profiles in this book have been broken down into the following fact-filled sections: At a Glance, Overview, and Interview. Each offers a distinct perspective on the job, and taken together give you a full view of the job in question.

At a Glance

Each entry starts out with an At a Glance box, offering a snapshot of important basic information to give you a quick glimpse of that particular job, including salary, education and experience, personal attributes, requirements, and outlook.

- *Salary range.* What can you expect to make? Salary ranges for the jobs in this book are as accurate as possible; many are based on the U.S. Bureau of Labor Statistics' *Occupational Outlook Handbook*. Information also comes from individuals, actual job ads, employers, and experts in that field. It's important to remember that salaries for any particular job vary greatly depending on experience, geographic location, and level of education.
- *Education/Experience.* What kind of education or experience does the job require? This section will give you some information about the types of education or experience requirements the job might call for.
- *Personal attributes.* Do you have what it takes to do this job? How do you think of yourself? How would someone else describe you? This section will give you an idea of some of the personality characteristics and traits that might be useful to you if you choose this career. These attributes were collected from articles written about the job, as well as recommendations from employers and people actually doing the jobs, working in the field.
- *Requirements.* Are you qualified? You might as well make sure you meet any health, medical, or screening requirements before going any further with your job pursuit.

✅ *Outlook.* What are your chances of finding a service-related job? This section is based in part on the *Occupational Outlook Handbook*, as well as on interviews with employers and experts. This information is typically a "best guess" based on the information that's available right now, including changes in the economy, situations in the United States and around the world, job trends, and retirement levels. These and many other factors can influence changes in the availability of jobs in the service sector.

Overview

This section will give you an idea of what to expect from the job. For most of these unusual jobs, there really is no such thing as an average day. Each day is a whole new adventure, bringing with it a unique set of challenges and rewards. This section will give you an idea of what a person in this position might expect on a day-to-day basis.

The overview also gives you more details about how to get into the profession, offering a more detailed look at the required training or education, if needed, and providing an in-depth look at what to expect during that training or educational period.

No job is perfect, and **Pitfalls** takes a look at some of the obvious and maybe not-so-obvious pitfalls of the job. Don't let the pitfalls discourage you from pursuing a career; they are just things to be aware of while making your decision.

For many people, loving their job so much that they look forward to going to work every day is enough of a perk. **Perks** looks at some of the other perks of the job you may not have considered.

What can you do now to start working toward the career of your dreams? **Get a**

Jump on the Job will give you some ideas and suggestions for things that you can do now, even before graduating, to start preparing for this job. Opportunities include training programs, internships, groups and organizations to join, as well as practical skills to learn.

Interview

In addition to taking a general look at the job, each entry features a discussion with someone who is lucky enough to do this job for a living. In addition to giving you an inside look at the job, this interview provides valuable tips for anyone interested in pursuing a career in the same field.

APPENDIXES

Appendix A (Associations, Organizations, and Web Sites) lists places to look for additional information about each specific job, including professional associations, societies, unions, government organizations, training programs, forums, official government links, and periodicals. Associations and other groups are a great source of information, and there's an association for just about every job you can imagine. Many groups and associations have a student membership level, which you can join by paying a small fee. There are many advantages to joining an association, including the chance to make important contacts, receive helpful newsletters, and attend workshops or conferences. Some associations also offer scholarships that will make it easier to further your education.

In **Appendix B (Online Career Resources)** we've gathered some of the best general Web sites about unusual jobs in the service sector, along with a host of very specific Web sites tailored to individual service sector jobs. Use these as a springboard to your own Internet research. Of course, all of this information is current as we've written this book, but Web site addresses do change. If you can't find what you're looking for at a given address, do a simple Internet search—the page may have been moved to a different location.

READ MORE ABOUT IT

In this back-of-the-book listing, we've gathered some helpful books that can give you more detailed information about each job we discuss in this book. Find these at the library or bookstore if you want to learn even more about service jobs.

AAA HOTEL RATER

OVERVIEW

For almost 100 years, the American Automobile Association (AAA) TourBook has helped generations of leisure travelers find the perfect overnight hotel rooms and excellent restaurants by providing details on pricing, amenities, and location—not to mention that all-important AAA rating.

AAA is a nonprofit organization of more than 100 motor clubs serving more than 40 million members in the United States and Canada—one of the largest travel organizations in the world. The AAA TourBooks are grouped by single states or geographical areas (such as "Mid-Atlantic" or "Florida"), and lists attractions, lodgings, and restaurants. Each hotel listing is selected only after a thorough, unannounced evaluation by a AAA hotel inspector, and each hotel is given a "diamond" rating—one through five. If you've ever wondered where those ratings come from—they're the result of painstaking, thorough annual inspections by a team of full-time hotel inspectors who each visit at least 800 hotels a year.

To be considered for approval and rating by AAA, hotels must first apply for an evaluation to determine if they meet the 27 basic lodging requirements expected by AAA members. If the application is approved by AAA, one of their highly trained, professional evaluators will visit the hotel. All evaluations are unannounced to ensure that the raters experience a hotel just as a AAA member would.

AAA first began including accommodation information in its travel publica-

AT A GLANCE

Salary Range

Salaries start at $30,000 to $40,000, although where the rater is located and the cost of living affects this rate. After five years, you can expect between $35,000 and $50,000 depending on your performance.

Education/Experience

You should have good computer skills so you can complete reports; some writing ability is helpful, as you must provide descriptive text to restaurants, attractions, and some hotels. AAA looks for skills, experience, and education that match the role of an AAA inspector.

Personal Attributes

AAA raters should have excellent communication and interpersonal skills, an interest in travel, attention to detail, and a strong sense of honesty.

Requirements

After a new rater is hired, he or she is sent for training at the AAA national office in Florida for several weeks. Next, the new AAA rater conducts visits with an experienced rater in the field for several more weeks. When the trainers and regional managers have decided the candidate can successfully evaluate and rate properties, he or she is then assigned a territory.

Outlook

Fair. With only 65 inspectors nationwide, there aren't a lot of jobs available at any given time with AAA, but there is some attrition as raters leave for other jobs or retire.

tions in the early 1900s; in 1937, the first field inspectors fanned out over the country to inspect hotels, motels, and restaurants. Twenty-six years later, AAA started rating lodgings as "good," "very good," "excellent," and "outstanding," bringing in the diamond rating system in 1977 during AAA's

Miles Taylor, AAA hotel rater

Miles Taylor had worked in restaurant management for 23 years and as an area manager for a restaurant chain for 12 years before becoming a AAA hotel rater. "Prior experience with planning and managing my time with numerous locations and working closely with general managers fit well with the responsibility of a tourism editor," he explains. "Part of my job in restaurants revolved around evaluating cleanliness, maintenance, service, and quality. Those same skills are used daily as a AAA rater." He'd been working in restaurants when Taylor responded to a help-wanted ad for a rater in his local paper.

On average, Taylor rates 18 to 20 hotels a week. Several variables come into play that determine the number of hotels he rates every day. "We rate all types of hotels," he says, "from small 20 to 30 unit motels that have very few public areas [no swimming pool, restaurant, breakfast room, or meeting room] to large full-service hotels with numerous restaurants, meeting rooms, fitness rooms, business centers, and more. The larger properties take more time to physically walk and rate." In addition, some of the hotels with full service require Taylor to evaluate and rate the services provided. "At those hotels we anonymously check in and stay overnight to evaluate all the services, from valet parking, concierge, bell service, room service, and more."

The amount of travel time required to reach each location and the nearby attractions also play a part in how many hotels can be rated each day, since raters also evaluate nearby attractions, restaurants, and campgrounds.

AAA raters have a territory for which they are responsible, and Taylor's territory consists of two entire states and parts of two others. He's responsible for rating and evaluating all the properties in his territory each year. Taylor decides which properties to visit each day and week, using good judgment and time management in planning how to complete his work by the deadline. "I enjoy the freedom to manage my time to maximize productivity," Taylor says. "I also enjoy assignments out of territory when we visit other parts of the country to conduct evaluations."

75th anniversary. The original goal of publishing its Diamond Ratings Guidelines was to standardize the rating process and ensure greater consistency, with precise guidelines as to what physical facilities, amenities, and services were expected at each rating level. The diamonds are an attempt to balance standards, because it's not easy to compare a 50-unit downtown historic inn to a 600-unit resort with a variety of accommodations and recreation choices.

The job of deciding which hotel gets how many diamonds goes to the AAA hotel rater. At the one- to three-diamond levels, AAA evaluates properties only based on the physical amenities: Is there a Jacuzzi? A meeting room? Internet capability? For these places, checklist-wielding hotel inspectors drop in at a AAA hotel unannounced, identify themselves, and start counting up the points. After the inspection, the inspector takes a few minutes to discuss the results, the rating, and any other relevant matters with the property owner or manager. This meeting won't raise the rating and should not in any way affect the AAA listing, but it can help the manager understand how the property fared—and why.

It's a slightly more challenging picture at the luxury level, where the difference

I enjoy meeting general managers and seeing the changes and progress in the industry. Another enjoyable part of our job is to dine and rate restaurants that range from fine dining to counter service restaurants."

It sounds like a lot of fun, but Taylor has also discovered what many people do who must travel constantly for work—after a while, all that travel just gets old. "Traveling weekly is not as exciting as many may think, and it can be the least enjoyable part of my job," he says. "Packing and unpacking, checking in and out of hotels, and driving for long distances can be tiresome and is nothing like traveling on vacation."

If all this sounds like a wonderful job to you and you're just dying to get out there and rate hotels, Taylor advises that you make certain you know everything about the job. Travel might seem like fun, but you really should enjoy the less glamorous parts of the job, he says. "A big part of rating hotels is delivering news the property owner may not want to hear, thoroughly checking rooms, bathrooms, and public areas for cleanliness and well-maintained furnishings. Traveling alone is also not for everyone and nothing like vacation, so make sure you are willing to make that sacrifice."

Even more difficult, he says, is being away from loved ones for short and long periods of time. "On the road, dining by yourself, unable to share sights, have conversation, and spend time with someone you care about is the most difficult part of the job," he says. "Sometimes the AAA rating the hotel receives is less than they had hoped. Sometimes a hotel is not approved for varying reasons. Delivering that disappointing news can often be very difficult."

Travel notwithstanding, most AAA raters say they love their job. "I have visited some attractions that I probably would not have known about or had the opportunity to visit if not for my work with AAA," Taylor says. "Museums, art galleries, historic locations, and zoos have been fun and educational and definitely an enjoyable part of the job."

between an average or an outstanding rating can come down to such details as the number of coat hangers in a hotel room closet. For these top-rated hotels, the inspector first checks out the physical aspects of the entire property, including exterior building and grounds, public areas, room decor and ambiance, guest room amenities, bathrooms, housekeeping, and maintenance. Then AAA sends its inspectors underground to actually stay incognito at the property. The review begins when the inspector calls to make a reservation. Is the hotel's reservations clerk friendly, polished, and professional? Does the clerk use proper language, such as "my pleasure"? The reservations clerk should also ask about special needs, offering to make dinner reservations or spa appointments if the property has such amenities.

Once the inspector arrives, the doorman should welcome the guest and quickly call her by name. (How? By quickly reading the guest's name off a luggage tag.) The doorman should try to use the guest's name at least three times before leading her to the front desk for check-in. Once registration is complete, the bellhop takes over, and is expected to use the guest's name while making friendly conversation on the way to the room, attending to every need along the way.

Next, the inspector reviews the cleanliness of the guest room, which must include enclosed closets with at least eight open-hook wood hangers, high-grade furniture (such as an armoire enclosing the television), and a luxurious bathroom with lots of soaps and shampoos.

It doesn't stop there. Inspectors must also check to make sure the top-rated hotels are keeping up with modern technology, offering high-speed Internet access and CD players with CDs in the rooms. During their stay, inspectors check the quality of the food, service, linens, china, and meal presentation of room service and the hotel's restaurant. While a hotel restaurant doesn't have to meet all the standards of a four-diamond restaurant, it should support the lodging's rating.

The services experienced by the field inspector must also support a top rating in order to achieve this level. AAA typically gives its 65 inspectors more flexibility in figuring out the final rating of top hotels. In most cases, the inspectors have decided whether the hotel has earned four or five diamonds by the time they check out, and they inform management of the results. A computerized worksheet calculates points won and lost, and the cumulative result is the hotel's rating—somewhere between one and five diamonds.

The AAA Five Diamond Award is the most coveted symbol of excellence for lodgings and restaurants and is presented only to those establishments that consistently offer world-class facilities, services, and amenities. For a hotel, being awarded the coveted AAA "five diamonds" is sort of like winning a gold medal at the Olympics. Fewer than half of 1 percent of the more than 36,000 lodgings and restau-

rants inspected and listed annually in the TourBook guides earn AAA's highest honor. In fact, only five lodgings in the country have received the Five Diamond Award every year since it was introduced in 1977: Marriott's Camelback Inn Resort and Golf Club Spa in Scottsdale, Arizona; The Broadmoor in Colorado Springs, Colorado; C Lazy U Ranch in Granby, Colorado; The Greenbrier in White Sulphur Springs, West Virginia; and the Four Seasons Hotel Vancouver.

So deciding on diamonds is the job of the AAA inspector, who tries to look at a hotel from a traveler's point of view. If you're handing over $400 or $500 a night for a room, you have a right to certain expectations. Your guest experience should be outstanding not just because the room is beautiful, but because the staff are thoughtful and genuine, and the service fluid, friendly, and prompt.

Of course, no single problem will be responsible for removing a diamond, and how a problem is handled can be just as important as whether there isn't a problem at all. For example, if an inspector is served a plate of steamed clams with one unopened clam—that's not good. But if the inspector's complaint brings the chef to the table to apologize followed by a free after-dinner drink as a consolation—that would probably be enough to make up for the original lapse. No place is perfect—so it's how problems are handled that can make the difference between getting that elusive extra diamond.

No matter how many diamonds a property racks up, sometimes an owner disagrees with an inspector's decision. Inspectors try very hard to keep personal bias out of the rating decision, but a person's level of knowledge and experience can influence the ultimate decision. Properties can appeal if they think their ratings are too low. AAA has an internal committee to review and resolve appeals from lodging, restaurant, and campground operators, weighing each case individually.

AAA also tracks complaints it receives about properties from members. If a property receives a number of bad marks and doesn't try to fix the issue after receiving a warning, AAA will drop it from the rating system. The hotel can't reapply to be rated for at least two years.

Pitfalls

The number-one pitfall of this job, AAA raters agree, is the endless travel. While it may be glamorous and exciting at first, eventually the travel can become tedious and you start missing your family and friends. Raters usually have territories that cover several states, so that's a lot of driving around and a lot of nights away from home. It can also be difficult to have to look a hotel manager in the face and announce a poor rating, or the loss of a diamond.

Perks

While the everyday travel can be burdensome, there are fun aspects to the job, and one of the best is eating in some fabulous restaurants—on the house. It's all part of the job. Raters also enjoy considerable freedom in setting their schedule and determining which properties they visit when, and how many. As long as they meet their deadline, they're free to accomplish that any way they like.

Get a Jump on the Job

A background in the food service or hotel industry is very helpful for this job, so get a summer or weekend job at a restaurant or hotel as early as you can. Consider a hotel management major in college.

AMERICAN SIGN LANGUAGE INTERPRETER

OVERVIEW

A sign language interpreter working at a public gathering, church service, or community event can be fascinating to watch, and the graceful visual language truly beautiful. But for deaf individuals, sign language fulfills a vital communication role. There's a real need for well-trained experts in American Sign Language (ASL) to interpret between the hearing world and the community of deaf and hard-of-hearing individuals.

When you interpret, you must first hear and understand each thought, and then sign it, while keeping your own thoughts and opinions totally out of the picture. Your goal is to make the communication experience as complete as possible for both participants. Of course, interpreting involves more than just signing. Becoming fluent in ASL is just like learning any other language, with its own grammar and rules, its own slang, and the tendency to evolve over time. But ASL is also a visual language, which means that you use your facial expressions and body movements to help you convey what you want to say. Although it's possible to sign without using your face or body, you may confuse your deaf listeners this way, and your signing will look unnatural.

Becoming an ASL interpreter involves a lot more than simply learning a second language. Many people are able to master two languages and become fluently bilingual without ever learning to interpret, which involves an entire additional set of skills. To

become an interpreter, you must master the skill of interpreting as well as learning another language. What does that mean? First of all, when you interpret, both languages must be held in your consciousness at the same time, with constant interaction between the two. And that can be exhausting.

To understand the interpreting process a bit better, try listening for a few minutes to a simple political speech on TV—something that uses common, everyday vocabulary. Now, try to repeat everything the speaker is saying. You'll soon realize this isn't easy. Now imagine you're trying to repeat what the speaker is saying in another language.

When you're interpreting from English to ASL, you must analyze the grammar, syntax, and vocabulary of English, reconstruct an equivalent in ASL that matches the mood, inflection, tone, and cultural perspective of the speaker—and all while the English speaker is still speaking. This means you have to be listening to the new material while you're also reconstructing and signing what's already been said.

An interpreter must accurately convey messages between two different languages, which involves a skill that takes time to develop. It's also important to remember, however, that you're an interpreter, not an advisor: you've got to follow a strict code of ethics, and you can't interfere, advise, or interject personal opinions into interpreted situations.

The first step towards becoming an interpreter is to become fluent in ASL, either by signing continually with deaf relatives at home, or by taking classes at college, clubs, or local agencies, or adult education courses in the local public school system. Once you learn the basics, you can practice your signs with deaf people. Just as you can't become a fluent conversationalist in French or German overnight, fluency in ASL takes time, too; acquiring conversational skills in ASL is a learning process that never ends. To pick up enough signs for basic communication and to sign comfortably typically takes

one or two years, unless you're slower at picking up signs.

Once you've learned ASL, you've got to learn how to interpret by taking formal instruction in the skills and protocols of the interpreting process. Most community colleges and four-year universities have excellent interpreter training programs.

While formal training or a college degree isn't strictly required to become an interpreter, these courses are really helpful. Most likely, in the future, formal classes in interpreting will be a mandatory prerequisite for getting a national certification. Because interpreters must be able to handle many different situations and a wide range of vocabulary and subject material, the more education you have, the better you'll be able to deal with this material.

To be certified, you must be able to quickly figure out the preferred communication mode and sign style of a deaf client, and be able to use sign language, finger spelling, and facial expression to convey a message spoken in English. You must be able to use linguistically and visually correct principles and translate a message from a deaf client in sign language into grammatically correct English. You must also be able to distinguish between American Sign Language (ASL) and Signed English, and to provide interpreting or transliterating as appropriate.

It's a good idea to start out your career interpreting on a team, with a more experienced mentor. This way, you can work for a five- or ten-minute shift and then observe how the more experienced interpreter handles all aspects of the situation, from determining the appropriate selection of language, vocabulary, and technique to issues of ethics.

As technology changes, so too does interpreting. With the popularity of video relay service, deaf and hard-of-hearing customers can connect with telephone callers via videophone systems. This has provided

Doug Dunn, American Sign Language interpreter

Doug Dunn has been providing professional sign-language interpreting services professionally since October 1972, and informally since childhood. Today, he works mostly in the San Diego area. Born and raised in southern California, Doug began learning American Sign Language (ASL) as a child, from deaf friends; his first wife also was a deaf person who used ASL.

"[Back in the 1960s,] paid professional interpreting was very rare," Dunn says. "Only in court were interpreters paid, and even then people often brought friends or relatives instead of paying a professional. Looking back from the perspective of today's world, it seems hard to imagine," he says. "[Cal State University at Northridge] developed the first large-scale integrated mainstream program by a major university and I happened to be a student there at the time, so when they were overwhelmed by deaf registrants and had to recruit more interpreters, I just happened to be in the right place at the right time and got my first paid job in October 1972. Prior to that I never imagined anyone would ever pay for interpreting and even now sometimes I just can't believe what a great job I have and what a great career I've been so fortunate to be able to enjoy. It was a great part-time job for a student and I didn't even have to leave campus. Plus, I got staff parking!"

When national certification became available through the Registry of Interpreters for the Deaf (RID), he obtained the Comprehensive Skills Certificate, which in those days encompassed all other certifications. Subsequently, he got his Level 5 in 1983. He is also certified by the American Consortium of Certified Interpreters.

Once he moved to San Diego County in 1991, he moved into community interpreting through community organizations such as Greater Los Angeles Council on Deafness (GLAD), the Deaf Community Services of San Diego (DCS), and Network Interpreting Service. He also interprets for the court and for many private clients.

"During most of my career, interpreting has not been a viable profession," he explains. For most of his working life, he always had other business activities and he fitted his interpreting in between. "Only in the last decade has interpreting become a viable profession from which one could earn a good living," he says. "I always expected to work as an interpreter, and still plan to do so as long as I remain physically and mentally healthy, but I didn't expect it to become a viable stand-alone career as it fortunately has."

Over the years, he's owned and operated a communications service called Word Wizards, which deals with publishing and other communications. "Being self employed gave me the flexibility to also maintain a substantial number of interpreting hours," he says. "In recent years I have increased the mix of interpreting so that now it is more than 90 percent of my activity, and I can delegate Word Wizards to others."

The hardest part of interpreting, he says, are the unpredictable hours and scheduling difficulties, but the variety of work makes it all worthwhile. "I like best the variety of experiences I get exposed to," he says. "The worst are the jails, emergency rooms, mental hospitals, and drug rehab facilities. The best are the banquets, seminars, and standing onstage next to famous entertainers and leaders, including several U.S. presidents and foreign heads of state."

a sudden demand for top interpreters in areas where service centers are opening. Video interpreting requires interpreters who can be prepared for any situation without advance notice. When an incoming call arrives, the interpreter doesn't know where in the country the call is coming from, the level of the signer's education, or the person's signing style preferences. Most likely, the interpreter won't even know the deaf consumer. The subject material could range from highly technical to deeply personal—or maybe the caller just wants to order a pizza. As an interpreter on a video relay system job, you've got to be ready for anything.

Once you've learned how to interpret, you may decide to set up your own interpreting business, or you may choose to work for a company that provides interpreters for different settings. If you work as a staff interpreter, you'll usually be required to accept whatever assignments you're given. Working for a school, a court system, or an agency will limit the kinds of jobs you get to what that organization does. In other words, if you work for the courts, you'll be only interpreting in legal situations. On the other hand, you'll have a steady job, a regular paycheck, and benefits, and you don't have to handle taxes, licenses, and insurance. Working for a company is a good way to get started; this is also a good way for you to meet lots of people in the deaf community, which can help you eventually begin working as a freelance interpreter.

As a freelance interpreter, you may work with anyone you choose, including agencies, schools, courts, hospitals, and private clients. You may interpret for weddings, banquets, seminars on interesting subjects, and for celebrities or politicians, TV, and movies. On the other hand, you also may choose to handle more emotionally challenging jobs at jails, courts, police stations, hospital emergency rooms, and funerals.

Pitfalls

Interpreting is physically and mentally draining. As an interpreter, your job is to facilitate communication between those who don't share the same language. But this service is also highly intrusive; while deaf people want interpreters they often have mixed feelings about interpreters, and may resent the intrusiveness of the interpreting process. If you work as a freelance interpreter, you don't get benefits such as health insurance and vacation pay— and if you don't work, you don't get paid.

Perks

It can be enormously satisfying to help individuals who cannot understand each other's language communicate, and to help individuals who are deaf deal with the hearing world. Every day is different and you see many aspects of the community that you might not otherwise have experienced.

Get a Jump on the Job

You should take as many workshops and classes as possible to increase your signing skills. Practice with deaf and hard-of-hearing people often to improve your receptive skills. Check out the Registry of Interpreters for the Deaf, which maintains an online list of interpreting training programs. In addition to taking classes, you may want to check out books or videos about signing. While you can certainly learn ASL without going to a class, it isn't possible to master any language without using it as part of your daily life. If you want to become fluent in sign language, you must have deaf people in your life so you can communicate daily. If you already have deaf friends or relatives, then use sign language with them. If not, find out (perhaps from your ASL instructor, or through a local deaf services agency) a good place to meet deaf people, in a social setting or in an organization such as a civic group, political organization, church, or club with deaf members. Keep in mind that some deaf people are impatient with beginning sign language students, while others are very supportive and will give you encouragement and positive feedback. The combination of informal, natural interaction using the language plus formal classroom instruction will help you learn much more quickly.

AQUARIUM MAINTENANCE SERVICE PROVIDER

OVERVIEW

If you've ever been mesmerized by that tank of guppies in your doctor's office as they circle the tank, in and out of the seaweed and the little castle, you've already discovered the truth behind those studies showing fish have a calming and relaxing effect on people, even lowering blood pressure and stress levels. Maybe that's why many medical offices, hospitals, corporate headquarters, and shopping malls feature large tanks of brightly colored fish. Some even go so far as to incorporate fishponds into their landscaping.

While the tanks are a great amenity for customers and clients, more often than not the office staff doesn't have the knowledge or even the interest in maintaining a tank. For that reason, most of these tanks are maintained by businesses specializing in aquarium maintenance, offering everything from design, set-up, and regular maintenance to moving services if the office relocates.

Quite often, the process begins when a client contacts an aquarium specialist or aquarium maintenance service because they want a tank designed for their office or home. While sometimes a customer will have something specific in mind, quite often they leave it up to pros to design the tank. This is fun for the aquarium specialists, because they get a chance to design a tank that they might not be able to af-

AT A GLANCE

Salary Range

Salaries depend on whether the service provider owns the business, but employees' salary should range from $7.50 to $12 an hour. Business owners earn much more.

Education/Experience

Requirements depend on individual employers. Some positions or employees may have no educational minimums or requirements, while others may prefer or require a college degree. Individuals considering opening an aquarium maintenance business may want to consider classes in business-related topics, including management, accounting, and marketing.

Personal Attributes

Individuals offering aquarium maintenance need to be customer-oriented with good people skills. They should be hardworking and able to work well without constant supervision. They need to be able to take precise measurements and readings. It may help if they are enthusiastic and passionate about what they do. Physically, people who maintain and service aquariums need to be able to move large, very heavy tanks (with assistance), as well as carry equipment and other materials and supplies.

Requirements

Individuals who are self-employed or run a small business will most likely need to file Doing Business As (DBA) papers and tax forms, and acquire any other permits required under local and/or state ordinances. They may also be required to carry insurance and be bonded.

Outlook

Good. The interest in keeping fish and the healthful, relaxing benefits of watching fish tanks should ensure a steady need for tank maintenance.

ford or simply don't have room for in their own office or home. This also gives them a chance to work with many different types of fish and plants.

Norm Osimani, aquarium maintenance service provider

Norm Osimani started out in life as a chemist, but after a departmental layoff sent him to the help-wanted ads, he got a job working at a friend's pet store to get some hours in between job interviews. Six years later, he went into business for himself, establishing AquariClean, a business offering aquarium setups and maintenance. He's been happily running the business ever since, working with clients and overseeing a staff of installers and maintenance providers. In fact, his background in chemistry comes in handy as he's called upon to do all kinds of water testing and manipulating of chemicals.

In the beginning, Osimani says he and his partner were running around in a car, storing things in his partner's basement, trying to make a dollar. "Now that the business is more than five years old, my employees do all the rough stuff," he says, "and I'm relegated to sales and large installations of 500 gallons and above."

AquariClean is set up much like a retail pet shop, with a consulting room, a fish room, and lots of pictures to help customers get ideas about types of coral and fish. The company doesn't build the tanks themselves, however. "We deal with a few different manufacturers who build to our specifications," he says. "We give them the dimensions and they have engineers to help them figure out the thickness of the glass, the bond. We take delivery of the aquarium, put it in place, install the filters, and maintain the tanks."

Maintenance means that at the very least, someone from the company must visit a tank once a month to clean the aquarium, test the water, do maintenance, and change 20 percent of the water. "Some customers prefer that we come every week or every two weeks," he says, "but once a month is the minimum."

Filtration systems have come a long way in 10 to 15 years, but it doesn't take care of everything. "Fish actually excrete ammonia as waste, and that is broken down into less toxic compounds. However, over the course of four weeks, that end product of fish waste builds up. While we remove some of the water, we're vacuuming up the bottom at the same time, diluting the end product."

If working with fish and aquariums seems like an ideal job, Osimani suggests that you work hard, keep your mind open to possibilities, and foster your imagination. "Anything is possible," he says. "I didn't have this figured out until I was 30 years of age! Keep your nose to the grindstone and good things will happen."

His business is primarily residential, although about 40 percent of the aquariums are sold to businesses. "I like best that we're not stuck in cubicles," he says. "We get to be out on the road, although that's not so much fun in the winter in Chicago when it's snowing. But 99 percent of the people who are pet owners are salt of the earth. The people are great, the work's not difficult, and you get to deal with aquariums every day. What could be better?"

Once the tank is designed, the aquarium maintenance person installs it and gets it up and running; most of the time, the aquarium maintenance service will also then maintain the tank on a regular basis. This includes running chemical checks on the water (since too much or too little of certain chemicals can kill fish and plants).

The service will also clean the tank, which means raking and vacuuming the gravel, changing the water in the tank, cleaning or changing the filters as necessary, and also cleaning the exterior of the tank. Maintenance also includes checking everything to make sure that the equipment is running properly, and making any necessary adjustments or repairs. The only thing someone at the home or business will have to do to maintain the fish is to feed them. (And even then, the maintenance service may check the supply of food, and deliver it when supplies run low.)

In addition, most aquarium maintenance services offer emergency coverage 24 hours a day, seven days a week, including nights and weekends. Imagine a customer raiding the fridge for a late night snack, or working in the office over the weekend, and discovering a leaking filter or a seal gone bad. No customer is going to want to wait until morning, much less wait over the weekend until Monday morning, to have the tank repaired.

If you love fish and enjoy working with the public, a job providing aquarium maintenance might be an enjoyable way for you to make a living. When you first start, you'll probably need to work for someone else. If you're willing to work hard and learn, you'll gain valuable experience you can carry over into your own personal tanks at home or take with you to other jobs. You probably won't want to work cleaning fish tanks forever, and there are many options in this business. After getting some experience, you could open an aquarium maintenance service of your own, or you might combine the maintenance service with a retail fish store. You might get very interested in a few specific types of fish, and become a breeder. You might even go on to earn a degree in biology and maybe an advanced degree in a particular branch of biology, such as marine science, and take your training and education and work with tanks in zoos and public aquariums.

Pitfalls

Aquarium maintenance providers usually offer 24/7 emergency services, including weekends and holidays, which means a lot of hours. It may be difficult to make a full-time living in rural or small suburban areas, so relocating might be necessary. And, as with all service-related industries, dealing with customers can be very stressful.

Perks

Someone doing aquarium maintenance will have the opportunity to maintain a show-quality tank without the cost. You can meet interesting people while servicing the tanks, and share your interest in fish with others.

Get a Jump on the Job

If you're new to the world of fish and aquariums, be prepared to learn a massive amount of information. There are also many, many books available, some of which are so specific that they might only cover one certain species of fish from one certain lake. The Internet offers another huge source of information, with articles, information pages, forums, and chat rooms dedicated to any fish-related topic you can imagine. Learn as much as you can about different species of fish and plants. Then set up and maintain your own aquarium. Look for a job working at a fish store. If the store offers aquarium maintenance services, try to work your way into a position doing that type of work. Consider taking classes in biology, business, advertising, accounting, and marketing in high school or at a local junior or community college.

BEER TAP CLEANER

OVERVIEW

A customer goes to a restaurant, orders a beer, enjoys a meal—who ever thinks very hard about the details behind having that beverage arrive at the table cold and foamy? In fact, beer is a highly perishable beverage that can quickly deteriorate if not maintained in the correct way. Part of that proper maintenance is to make sure that the lines bringing the beer from the keg to the tap are immaculately clean.

In fact, it's so important that every state has passed laws mandating exactly how the lines should be kept clean, just as every other food handling–related issue is controlled by the government. Most states have laws requiring that draft beer lines must be cleaned at least once a week; a few states (such as Massachusetts) mandate twice-weekly cleanings.

It's important that beer lines be cleaned so as to remove a scale called calcium oxalate, commonly referred to as *beerstone*, which forms on the fittings, lines, and taps. If not completely removed during cleaning, beerstone leaves an unsanitary surface that can encourage the growth of germs that could find its way into the beer and make customers sick.

In addition, the germs can cause off-flavors or shorten the beer's shelf life. Line cleaning with the proper equipment and chemical eliminates the build-up of beerstone, protecting the integrity of the product. In addition, a few missed cleanings can cause the faucet and coupler to lock up and break.

As a result, any establishment with at least one beer tap must hire a beer tap

cleaner, who arrives each week to clean the lines using chemicals developed specifically for the brewing industry (sanitizers don't clean, and detergents in the line would kill a beer's head).

Beer lines can be short—just two feet away from the keg, if the keg is kept right under the bar. But some places have a line 60 or 80 feet away because the keg is kept in the walk-in cooler way back behind the kitchen. Because the lines have to be emptied of beer before they're cleaned each week, the cleaner might waste a gallon of beer for each line. Basically, the beer tap cleaner hooks up a line for the chemicals where the beer line would hook up, and pumps it through the faucet. The chemical flushes the line, and then it's rinsed out with water. Finally, the beer line is reconnected.

Rondell Light, beer tap cleaner

Rondell Light was looking for a business when he heard about a fellow wanting to sell his beer tap cleaning business in Reading, Pennsylvania. The customer base had dwindled to only about five customers by the time Light bought the business, because the owner drank some of the beer at every bar he went to. "You've got to know what you're doing," Light says. "You've got to have a straight head, and you can't drink while you're doing it. Some people say to me: 'Man, I'd like to have your job!' because they think it means I get to drink at every stop I make," Light says. "But if you have 40 or 50 accounts, if you drink at each one, at the end of the day you're drunk. You can't get your work done."

Within three and a half years, he's built the business up to 32 customers. Because state law requires beer taps to be cleaned weekly, there's always plenty of work—and only about three other competitors in his area.

The basic process that Light uses is fairly simple. "Beer gets a milky buildup if it's exposed to air, around the fittings at the faucet and where the tap hooks up," Light says. "It turns into something like tar—it gets gunky. It's not healthy, and customers can get sick from drinking beer from a bad line.

"Years ago they used to pump glass beads through the lines, followed by tiny sponges," he says. "That's kind of a primitive method, because it used to nick the lines and provide more area for yeast and bacteria to build up. That's what tap cleaning does—eliminate the buildup."

Companies with only one beer tap can be cleaned quickly, but some places have many more lines. "I have some customers with as many as 45 lines," he says, "like the Reading Phillies. I'm there for a couple of hours when I clean their taps."

Because an average bar only has two taps, Light says, you don't make much money on each customer—but you come back each week to service those taps. Light charges $10 to $15 for cleaning two taps, depending on how far he has to drive to get there. "It's a guaranteed thing," Light says. "If you're loyal to your customers . . . you do so many a week, it adds up."

When he started out, Light bought the pump and a bucket of concentrate, paying almost $1,000 for each of his five customers. "I knew as long as I didn't lose those five customers—well, I did the math. If I put money back into it, I could easily pay for it within a year. I figured from there

Because the law requires that every beer tap must be cleaned regularly, a cleaner with a strong work ethic and lots of clients can keep busy just about around the clock.

Pitfalls

If you clean beer taps for a living, you've got to face the fact that you're going to smell like beer most of the time. You may also be required to carry lots of liability insurance to protect bar owners if you make a mistake and some customers get sick.

Perks

This is typically a one-person business, so if you like independence and running your own show, this could be the job for you. There is very little competition in general, since many people don't know about the job. Since legal requirements guarantee that beer lines must be cleaned, there is a continuous supply of work.

on out, it would be profit." If he managed to make the business grow, he'd be doing even better. "Basically it's a hidden little business, and not too many people know about it," he says.

Of course, there are expenses beyond the pump and the chemicals—and the biggest one is insurance. "Insurance kills me," he says. "I have a couple of customers that require a ridiculous amount. Reading Country Club wants me to have a million dollars general liability. If I don't do my job right, people could get sick. I use a harsh acid cleaner, and if I didn't clean it out of the lines, there could be problems. If I don't hook something up right, liquid is going to be everywhere. Or if I don't put it back right, taps could leak and damage the bar or the floors. The lines are pressurized, so there could be leaks."

Nevertheless, it's been a good business and Light works hard to continue to grow. In addition to cleaning taps, Light realized he could boost his business by offering parts as well, so he's equipped a van with some extras. "I have gaskets and O rings—little parts that can go wrong. I keep spare beer lines and air lines. I'm not just working out of the trunk of my car. I ran an ad in the Yellow Pages this year, listing the business as a 'full service draft company.' Yes, I clean and service the lines, but if you need parts or something breaks, I can fix it."

In fact, business is so good he thinks that in the future he might hire some employees to help him out, since he figures he can only add another 15 to 20 accounts without ending up with too much work. "There's only so much time in a day," he explains. "Sometimes my mornings start at 5:30 a.m., and I've got four or five of them done before 11 a.m."

You'd be surprised how many places offer draft beer and so require the services of a beer tap cleaner. "There's beer taps at more places than you think," he says. "Golf courses, night clubs, country clubs, little Italian clubs in town. Every little dive has a beer tap, and there's a lot of them in Reading. There could be five or six bars in one block."

"I like being able to be my own person," he says. "I'm a one-man business. Once you get your customers, there's very little overhead. Most is profit besides the insurance and the gas. It's possible if you get enough customers, you could make good money."

Get a Jump on the Job

You can't major in beer tap cleaning in college, but you can sign on as an apprentice if you can find a cleaner looking for help. It helps to know someone in the business. Some community colleges may offer courses not strictly on tap cleaning, but on the installation of pipes and service of refrigeration units.

BIKE MESSENGER

OVERVIEW

You see them racing perilously through crowded city streets in places like New York, San Francisco, or Washington, D.C. They often travel by bike with a backpack slung over their shoulders, a beeper strapped to their belts, and a cell phone tucked into their back pockets. Their mission: to deliver those papers, contracts, court filings, or medical specimens in record time so they can get to the next client and deliver more packages in record time.

Bike messengers are used by law firms, advertising agencies, architectural firms, government agencies, and graphic arts agencies. Many bike messengers are concentrated in New York, and, to a lesser extent, Washington D.C., San Francisco, Chicago, and Boston.

Although there may be a certain exhilaration born of speeding through crowded city streets, narrowly missing cars and pedestrians, being a courier is by no means an easy job. Local messengers—whether they travel by car, foot, bike, moped, cargo van, or box truck—are competing for an ever-shrinking parcel business. With the advent of e-mail, fax machines, and digital cameras, there just isn't the need to send so much paper flying across town in a backpack or the back of a truck for physical delivery. In addition, many overnight delivery services actually cost less than couriers.

As a result, bike messengers have seen a dramatic decline in their business, and those still zipping around city streets are making about half of what they made just 15 years ago. To make matters worse,

AT A GLANCE

Salary Range

Bike messengers usually earn somewhere between $15,000 and $33,000 a year. Bike messengers usually get paid by commission on each delivery, and some earn as little as 50 cents per delivery. Those working in New York typically make between $3 and $10 per delivery, depending on where and for whom they work. On a very busy day, a messenger might expect between 20 and 25 deliveries, but a slower day could mean far fewer deliveries.

Education/Experience

High school diploma or GED.

Personal Attributes

Excellent biking skills, ability to follow directions and work with minimal supervision. Messengers should also have stamina, reliability, speed, attention to detail, good work ethic, and ethical behavior.

Requirements

There are no requirements or certificates necessary for being a bike messenger, other than the ability to ride a bike in heavy traffic, but employers usually hire employees with good safety records, some experience, and reliability.

Outlook

Declining. The number of jobs for messengers is expected to grow very slowly through 2012, as technology makes it easier and easier to send information electronically instead of by hand. On the other hand, this is an occupation with a high turnover rate since it is stressful and dangerous trying to deliver documents quickly for low pay and without health insurance, so it will probably always be possible to find some work, at least in big cities. In any large city, there will probably always be at least six companies to work for, and six months of experience makes you a veteran—and in demand.

couriers are generally paid by commission. That means you're the one who usually has to cough up the money to buy yourself the appropriate gear—cell phones, bikes,

Kevin "Squid" Bolger, bike messenger

Kevin Bolger had never thought too much about becoming a bike messenger like his older brother. "Nobody ever told me about it when I was looking at career options at my college prep school in Queens!" he says. But one day, when his older brother broke his finger and quit the bike messenger job he'd had for a year, Bolger thought he'd grab the bike and give the job a try. He'd been working as a security guard at the time, and the idea of riding a bike for a living seemed refreshing.

"I thought I'd give it a shot," he recalls, and signed up with N.Y. Minute, a New York City messenger service. "It was a really cool company, and a really friendly bunch of people," he says. "Once I realized you really could make a living at this, it was great. I love being outside, getting exercise, and I really love being a part of New York City."

As all bike messengers know, there is a darker side to the business—zipping through the heavy downtown traffic can be hazardous to your health. "I've been hurt a few times," he says, "and I've attended about 15 memorials for messengers who've been killed over the years."

Now aged 34, he's been working for the past 14 years and says he feels better than ever. "I feel in better shape than when I started," he says, "and I guess I'll keep doing this until I find something I like better."

If the freedom and independence appeals to you and you'd like to try working as a bike messenger, Squid Bolger has one word of advice: wear your bike helmet. "Not everyone is cut out for this kind of job, but those who are really love it," he says. You can start practicing right now, by riding your bike as much as possible, because the better your biking skills the faster you can work and the safer you'll be.

"And what can be better than getting paid to ride your bike?" he asks.

helmets, gloves, insurance, and new inner tubes for blown bike tires. And serious couriers invest in two bikes, not one. You don't want to miss a couple of days of work when something breaks on your bike or if someone steals it.

Even so, couriers are never likely to become completely extinct, since there will always be certain items that can't be faxed or e-mailed, including medical specimens, parts and supplies, and original contracts. In larger cities, couriers often carry important contracts and checks from point A to point B. Couriers also often deliver corporate gifts, such as bottles of wine or theater tickets. And as more people use the Internet for shopping, couriers will be needed to deliver an expanding number of day-to-day items, such as groceries and medicines, to a wider audience.

On any given day, you'd bike to your first business and pick up documents, delivering them across town. As you do so, you must record each pick-up and delivery, recording mileage if you're paid by the mile. If you work for a courier company, the dispatcher decides which packages you get, and you get paid more for "emergency" deliveries rather than on how much they weigh. A good dispatcher will try and spread the high-paying jobs around fairly evenly, but it's always a good idea to try to be the dispatcher's best friend.

Some bike messengers work for private delivery companies, while others are self-employed. Although those who own their own businesses have more freedom, they are responsible for fixing their transportation, marketing their business, and taking care of all that paperwork.

Pitfalls

Being a bike messenger is a physical job, and a dangerous one, since you're usually working in relatively dense, congested, large cities with a strong business culture. As a courier, you will get hit by cars—it's considered an occupational hazard. Many couriers say that it's hard to work for a year straight without getting into an accident. Couriers don't earn a lot for all of their effort. There's also the risk of having your bike stolen, since just about any lock can be broken and if you lock the bike frame to the wheel, the whole thing can be thrown into a truck and removed, where the thief can pick the lock at his leisure.

Perks

One of the most appealing aspects of the courier lifestyle is the freedom. Few jobs offer as much freedom as does a bike messenger, flying through traffic in the best and worst of weather. Even if you work for a courier company, your bosses typically have neither the time nor the inclination to peer over your shoulder to watch you at work. Your only obligation is to get the packages to where they have to be, when they have to be there. As long as you do that, no one cares what else you do—and if you don't do it, you don't get paid. If it's a slow afternoon and you feel like hanging around outside the courier office drinking coffee, no one will ever come out and ask you if that is an appropriate way to spend company time. This job is usually stress free, you get to stay in great shape, and most of the people involved are friendly.

Get a Jump on the Job

The first thing you should do if you're thinking about being a bike messenger is to learn how to ride your bike safely. Then learn how to ride fast—because the quicker you can zip in and out of traffic and make your deliveries, the more deliveries you'll be able to make in a day and the more money you'll earn.

BODY PARTS MODEL

OVERVIEW

Close-up ads on TV or magazines for panty hose, hand cream, and nail polish showcase the elegant hand or leg of a successful body parts model—that's a model with a spectacular hand, foot, arm, or leg who is paid very well to have that particular body part highlighted. His or her face may be totally average, but a body parts model will have a specific body part that is standout, so as to best highlight the product: shoes, hose, gloves, handbags, jewelry, beauty products, fragrances, and cosmetics.

If you have a fine pair of hands and fingers, a beautiful set of legs and feet and toes, really healthy teeth or hair, a great neckline, good waist or hips, or a pair of beautiful eyes, you can be a parts model—even if you don't think you have the greatest looks in general.

In particular, hand models should have flawless, smooth skin on their hands, with no visible pores, and evenly shaped nails. The shape of the hands and nail bed is important. Men's hands should not be too hairy.

Leg models need to have legs that are smooth, long, and shapely. The skin of the legs should be free of veins, scars, and blemishes. Foot models should have feet with smooth skin tone and evenly shaped toes and nails, without any noticeable veins, corns, or other foot blemishes. The shoe size can range anywhere from a size 6 to a 10 for women, and a 7 to a 12 for men. There are even torso models, who can be men or women with even skin tone and a well-shaped body.

AT A GLANCE

Salary Range

Hours depend on how much you want to work and how good you are at your job; salary can range from a low of less than $10 an hour to more than $300 an hour; hourly earnings can be even higher for supermodels and others in high demand. However, work may be intermittent and jobs may last only a few hours. Almost all models work with agents, and pay 15 to 20 percent of their earnings in return for an agent's services. Most models must provide their own health and retirement benefits.

Education/Experience

No formal training is needed to be a body parts model, but models should be photogenic. Modeling schools provide training in posing and other basic tasks, but attending such schools does not necessarily lead to job opportunities. In fact, many agents prefer beginning models with little or no previous experience and discourage models from attending modeling schools and buying professional photographs.

Personal Attributes

You've got to have body parts that are both attractive and photogenic. The ability to relate to the camera in order to capture the desired look on film is essential. For TV or video work, parts models must be able to move their hands or legs (or whatever part is being photographed) gracefully and confidently. Models must be professional, polite, prompt, patient, and persistent. You'll also need to be able to maintain a rigorous self-care routine for the body part that you're modeling.

Requirements

An attractive physical appearance of the body part in question is necessary to become a successful body parts model. You'll need to be at least 18, with flawless skin with an even tone and perfect appearance of the part. Hands should have no wrinkles, lines, freckles, or other marks and no discernable muscle. Legs should be smooth, long, and lean, with no visible veins or scars; feet should

(continues)

AT A GLANCE (continued)

be smooth, supple, with no bunions or other misshapen parts; toenails or fingernails should be perfect. Any ethnic and racial background is permissible.

Outlook

Employment of body parts models is expected to grow about as fast as the average for all occupations through 2012. Body parts modeling is a glamorous occupation, with limited formal entry requirements, so if you want to be a body parts model, you can expect keen competition for jobs. The parts modeling profession typically attracts many more applicants than there are openings available. Only parts models that meet the unique requirements of the assignment will work regularly, but demand should continue to increase for models from diverse racial and ethnic groups. Nevertheless, most models experience periods of unemployment.

A model can either decide to work independently or with an organization or modeling agency. An independent or freelance model needs to track down assignments and follow up on nonexclusive contracts. Fashion centers of Europe offer excellent campaign opportunities and growth prospects for a modeling career. New York, Los Angeles, Chicago, and Miami are the American fashion modeling hubs.

Typically, a modeling agency doesn't hold an "open call" for parts models. Instead, you should send an agency pictures of the body part that you want to model (either color or black-and-white); they should be professionally lit and photographed. Unfortunately, snapshots and home photos just don't have the clarity of image and detail that an agency will need. The photographs can be no larger than 8

by 10 inches, and you should include your name, address, and all your telephone contact numbers. Girls and women should include age, height, bust, waist, hips, hair color, and eye color; boys and men should include age, height, weight, suit size, waist, inseam, shirt size, hair color, and eye color.

There aren't any standard poses, but if you're sending photos of your legs, you should include at least one full-length photo and another shot from the waist down.

For a hand model, photos can include two or three prints of one hand or both together. You'll also need to include your glove size (not "small," "medium," or "large," but the actual number of the glove size you wear) and also a ring size.

Foot models should send photos wearing sandals or barefoot, and include your shoe size.

During a photo shoot, a parts model poses to demonstrate the features of clothing or product that is being depicted in the ad. Models make small changes in posture to capture the look the client wants. As they shoot film, photographers instruct models to pose their hand, foot, or leg in certain positions and to interact with their physical surroundings. Models work closely with photographers, hair and clothing stylists, makeup artists, and clients to produce the desired look and to finish the photo shoot on schedule. Stylists and makeup artists prepare the model for the photo shoot, provide touch-ups, and change the look of models throughout the day. If stylists are not provided, models must apply their own makeup and bring their own clothing. Because the client spends time and money planning for and preparing an advertising campaign, the client usually is at the shoot to make sure the work is satisfactory.

Almost all parts models work through agents, who provide a link between models and clients. A model's agency is an important factor in ultimate success, since the better the agent's reputation and skill, the more assignments a model is likely to get. Because clients prefer to work with agents, it's very hard for a parts model to pursue a freelance career. Clients pay the models, and the modeling agency takes a portion of the model's earnings for its services. Agents scout for new faces, advise and train new models, and promote them to clients. Agents find and nurture relationships with clients, arrange auditions called *go-sees*, and book shoots if a model is hired. They also provide bookkeeping and billing services to models and may offer them financial planning services. Relatively short careers and high incomes make financial planning an important issue for successful models.

Because a model's success depends on previous work, development of a good portfolio is key to getting assignments. A portfolio is a collection of a model's previous work that is carried to all go-sees and bookings, and includes photographs and *tear sheets* (samples of a model's editorial print work). Tear sheets of actual jobs are the best, but great photos showing your body part in a variety of poses will show what you can do. The higher the quality and currency of the photos in the portfolio, the more likely it is that you'll find work. Your portfolio should include at least one photo clearly showing your face, not only to open up the possibility that you might get bookings to show your face on camera, but also so that the client knows who you are when you walk in for your body parts booking. A model also needs to put together a *comp card* that contains the best photographs from the portfolio, along with all relevant measurements.

With the help of their agents, models spend lots of time promoting and developing themselves, putting together their portfolios, printing composite cards, and traveling to go-sees. When a call comes in, the agent tells the model about the pay, date, time, and length of the shoot, and what product is being promoted and what image they should project. Some models research the client and the product being modeled to prepare for a shoot. Models use a document called a voucher to record the rate of pay and the actual duration of the job, which is used for billing purposes after both the client and model sign it. Once a job is completed, models must check in with their agency and plan for the next appointment.

Because a model's career depends on excellent physical characteristics, you must control your diet, get regular exercise, and stay healthy. Haircuts, pedicures, and manicures are necessary work-related expenses for parts models. Modeling can be hard work, involving long hours standing, walking, and posing in awkward positions. It also requires many hours of grooming each day. Being a parts model means you can't do strenuous chores or handle potent cleaning products if your hands are your meal ticket; you can't injure your foot, cut your leg, or get athlete's foot if you're a leg or foot model.

You'll also have to be very careful about monitoring your lifestyle. Hand models can never wash dishes or do housework without wearing rubber gloves. They can never use their nails to open a letter or open jars. Body parts models should get a paraffin wax treatment once a month, which can help restore suppleness and moisture to hands, legs, and feet, and take particular care of nails. You'll always need

Ellen Sirot, hand model

I never planned to be a hand model," says Ellen Sirot, currently one of the country's most successful hand models. "It was not my answer to the question 'What do you want to be when you grow up?'" Instead, Sirot fell into the field of parts modeling as a way to earn extra money while trying to support herself as a dancer. She began working as a leg and foot model.

"I quickly realized that modeling definitely beat waitressing," she says. But she recognized that the competition was fierce, and when she figured out that hand models snagged the most work, she realized she'd need to break into that tight market to make a full career of parts modeling.

"As I looked at my hands, I thought they were very nice," she admits. She'd been fairly successful pretty quickly in the leg and foot market, so she was surprised when her agent told her that although her hands were nicely shaped, they had to be perfect before she went on an audition.

At that point, she began her quest for perfect hands. "I was a hand detective, staring at everybody's hands, until I finally figured out that what the clients were looking for were hands with even skin tone that were soft, smooth, and unblemished." There should not be many wrinkles, the nails must be healthy—clear and strong, with supple, well-conditioned cuticles. She spent a year tracking down effective products and developing her own unique hand treatments. She wears one of her 100 pairs of white gloves during the day to prevent sun damage, and one of 100 pairs of elegant gloves at night just to be on the safe side. After all, she notes, the skin on your hands is as delicate as the skin on your eyelids. She also moisturizes at least 20 times a day and night. As she worked on her hands, they improved dramatically, and soon she was booking job after job. Over the last 12 years, her hands have continued to improve. "The skin of my hands is now softer than a baby's bottom," she says.

As a former dancer, she had excellent muscle memory, and she was able to hold positions for very long periods of time—an essential skill when doing hand modeling. It also means she's able to repeat movements, exactly the same way—another vital skill for a body parts model on TV. "On TV, it's all about the motion," she explains. "You have to be able to do a task smoothly, at the right angle." It calls for perfect gracefulness, and an awareness of muscle—exactly the skills perfected in a dancer.

to use sunscreen on skin and nails (both fingernails and toenails are susceptible to sun damage, including several types of skin cancer). An SPF of 15 or higher is good and will help aid against liver spots and premature aging. You'll also need to drench your skin with moisturizer before bed.

Pitfalls

Like any freelance job, if you don't work—you don't eat. The constant pressure of earning a paycheck—one that doesn't include benefits or paid vacation—can be taxing. Parts models must also be extremely flexible, able to drop what they're doing at a moment's notice to go out on an audition or a job. The work of a hand model can be glamorous, but it is far more often difficult.

You may need to work on location in a cold, damp outdoor location. Schedules can be demanding, and it can be stressful to be

Body parts models are divided into different types, and Sirot says she's a "healthy Mommy hand," which means she can be used to advertise products for around the home, as well as for jewelry and nail polish.

Since she began, Sirot's hands have been seen in hundreds of print ads and TV commercials, and in every major fashion magazine. She's worked with many of New York's top photographers, and is a frequent interviewee on *Entertainment Tonight, Eyewitness News, The Early Show,* and *Fox 5 News.* So well known is she on the parts model circuit that *Ladies Home Journal* dubbed her the "Cindy Crawford of hand and foot modeling."

Making a living with her hands means they need to be kept in tip-top shape, which means she's got to live a rather odd lifestyle. In summer she wears elbow-length gloves and avoids any weather conditions. In the past seven years, she has not touched a piece of paper, cleaned a dish or floor, taken out the garbage, or handled anything sharper than a butter knife. She tries not to immerse her hands in water at all, and because she can't build up her hand muscles, she can't play tennis.

"I treat my hands as precious treasures, thinking of their protection at all times," she says. "I'm incredibly careful." One paper cut or ragged cuticle can mean she's unemployable for weeks. In addition to protecting her hands, she must avoid using them in any way that would involve muscles, such as opening a window or carrying a heavy bag. To keep her feet toned, she avoids high heels, sleeps with her legs raised, and wraps her precious toes in plastic after moisturizing.

"My no-work hands are much in demand because they photograph very well, without vein, muscle, or bone bulges," she says. "The perfect hand for photography is almost dead looking, so pale, so un-built up." The hands should look hairless, poreless, and veinless.

Still, it may seem simple, but very few people are able to make a good living as a body parts model; most of the others model part time. "I've got a nice little niche," she says, "and you can't be overexposed. I can do a zillion hand or foot ads."

Of course, keeping her hands and feet looking perfect means her lifestyle is curtailed, and she's got to be available for last-minute jobs. "I keep all my time available for hand modeling jobs," she says. But because her hourly rate is so high, she only needs to work a day or two a week. "It's the best part-time job in the world," she says.

away from friends and family and needing to focus on the photographer's instructions despite constant interruption for touch-ups and set changes. Because modeling jobs are concentrated in New York, Miami, and Los Angeles, you'll have the best chance for work if you live in one of those cities.

Perks

Successful models interact with a variety of people and enjoy frequent travel. They may meet potential clients at several go-sees in one day and often travel to work in distant cities, foreign countries, and exotic locations.

Get a Jump on the Job

You can't start too soon to take care of your feet, hands, hair, or whatever body part you think you'd like to model. Read everything you can about parts modeling, and study ads on TV and in magazines and newspapers. Look at how the model placed the body part, what the part looks like. Compare your hands or feet to the models' photos and work on getting yours to look that good.

BRAILLE TRANSCRIBER

OVERVIEW

To a person who cannot see, learning the simple braille code of raised dots opens up whole new worlds of literature that would otherwise not be possible to explore. Yet without a braille transcriber, the pleasure of reading would be denied hundreds of thousands of blind readers. Some modifications have been made to it over the years but the braille code in use today is virtually the same as it was in 1834. Today, in virtually every language around the world, the code named after Louis Braille is the standard form of writing and reading used by blind people.

Braille dots are read by moving the index fingers of both hands from left to right along each line. Most blind individuals can read braille at about 125 words a minute, although speeds of up to 200 words a minute are possible. Braille readers can locate information, be more independent, protect their privacy, and participate more fully in their career and daily life. There are braille codes for all languages, for mathematics and science, and for music.

All text is represented by 63 characters called *braille cells,* which are all the possible arrangements of two side-by-side columns of three dots each. The dots within the cells are numbered 1 through 3 in the left column and 4 through 6 in the right column. The cells are embossed in horizontal lines across the page. There are usually 40 cells per line and 25 lines per page, on paper 11 inches high by 11.5 inches wide.

AT A GLANCE

Salary Range

$18,000 to $50,000+; fees depend upon the level of certification, previous experience, and the difficulty of the work assignment.

Education/Experience

To enroll in braille transcription training, you must have a high school diploma. The Library of Congress's National Library Services for the Blind and Physically Handicapped offers a free correspondence course. The National Library Service of the Library of Congress has a correspondence course which, when completed, leads to the first certification a professional transcriber needs (Literary Braille Transcriber). For more information, see Appendix A.

Personal Attributes

Braille transcribers typically enjoy working alone, and must be extremely picky and patient. Their work must be flawless, because braille readers are depending on the braille text to be perfect.

Requirements

There are both certified and uncertified transcribers who work in the field; uncertified people usually work under certified transcribers.

Outlook

The Americans With Disabilities Act was passed in 1990, giving Americans with disabilities the legal right to reasonable accommodations, making it clear that braille materials need to be available in hundreds of thousands of locations, such as banks, hotels, schools, and government meetings. Because government agencies and businesses have an urgent need for transcribers to prepare braille materials, it's a growing field. On the other hand, modern technology means that a textbook that once required 300 hours for a braille transcriber to two years ago may now only take 30 hours, which means one transcriber can do 10 times as many books.

The meaning of the cells depends on their context. For example, in Braille English the sign for *k* (dots 1 and 3) represents:

- the letter *k* when it is in contact with other letters within a word
- the word *knowledge* when it stands between two blank cells (spaces)
- the word *know* when it is preceded by a dot-5 cell and the two-cell sign stands between spaces
- the part-word *know* when it is preceded by a dot-5 cell and is in contact with other letters within a word.

The official braille code (*English Braille, American Edition*) is published by The Braille Authority of North America (BANA), which represents many agencies and consumer groups and has been responsible for updating and interpreting the basic literary braille code and the specialized codes for music, mathematics, and other codes in the United States and Canada. Other countries have similar authorities.

The establishment of the braille alphabet was a boon to people who couldn't see, but it also opened up jobs for individuals responsible for transcribing words into the special coded language. If you're looking for an interesting and rewarding career that requires just a small investment of time and money for training, braille transcription may be just what you're seeking.

Braille transcribers convert anything in print form into braille, which can then be read by those who are trained to decipher the code. There are several ways to transcribe into braille, using techniques ranging from manual methods to computer software-based conversions; learning the process takes about four months.

You can transcribe braille by simply substituting a braille character for its printed equivalent, but this type of charac-ter-by-character transcription (known as Grade 1 braille) is used only by beginners.

Until the advent of computers and electronic printers (called *embossers*), braille transcribers used Perkins Braillers to transcribe print material into braille. Today, transcribers use computers and electronic embossers with translation software, so that the individual can work on a computer screen in a print mode, and then press a button to translate the document to braille. The electronic file is then sent to an embosser for rapid single or multiple copy preparation. Because the source document was a hard copy book, each letter and symbol had to be entered by hand.

When scanners and OCR (optical character recognition) software became available, those using computers could be much more productive than those using a manual brailler. However, even with the best scanner and OCR package, there was still a lot of hand entry required. Once text and graphics have been transcribed, the bindings, covers, labeling, and packaging are completed.

Braille is used to produce just about anything a blind person might need to read, including educational and recreational reading and practical manuals, along with contracts, regulations, insurance policies, directories, appliance instructions, and cookbooks. Through braille, blind people can also read music scores, hymnals, playing cards, Scrabble boards, and other game boards.

Braille transcribers (both certified and noncertified) work with many different organizations who need certified transcribers, including public and private school systems, nonprofit organizations, independent living groups, universities, and corporations. If you're independent and you enjoy working at home, you can also find jobs as a self-employed transcriber.

Martha Cone, braille transcriber

Martha Cone has a Ph.D. in microbiology, but these days she spends her time encoding English into braille. "I stumbled upon braille transcription after I retired from my first career as a microbiologist," she explains, joining Braille Plus, Inc. in Salem, Oregon, in 2002 to work primarily as a tactile graphics specialist. The company produces materials in several alternate formats: braille, large print, audiotape, and diskette. However, she very quickly moved into braille transcription, and brings her experience in the sciences and mathematics to bear on braille math, called Nemeth Code. Cone just received her certification from the Library of Congress.

"My first experience with braille was producing graphics for a college calculus textbook," she says. "We produce 'tactile' graphics that can be read by touch. All the labels and numerical information in the print version of the graph are adapted for the tactile version." Cone explains that reproducing tactile graphics involves a blending of art and science. "It's not just a process of copying and pasting and then printing on a special machine," she says. "The spatial relationships have to work for perception by touch—things have to be farther apart and larger, and braille labels take up more room. Colors, line thicknesses, shadings, and so on have to be represented in a meaningful way."

She discovered that her calculus background is valuable in doing the math and science transcription. "I have learned the many symbols and how they are put together," she explains. "It just helps to have some exposure to a subject. It's like language: It is much easier for me to transcribe in English or German—two languages I have more exposure to—than in Spanish or French." This doesn't mean that one couldn't transcribe calculus without taking a calculus course, she points out. "But knowing a little about the subject just makes it go faster."

Cone often uses software to help her transcribe. "Like any software, the software is in the process of evolution," she says. "It does not work perfectly." For example, if you were using your computer's spell check option, and you typed *Spell Czech* it most likely would not flag the misused *Czech* because that is still a valid correctly spelled word—it's just not the right word for the sentence. In much the same way, braille produced by braille software always requires human oversight. "There is no such thing as 'push button braille' because things can always go wrong with software and with embossers [braille printers]. If there were not someone who knew what they were looking at, then the user would be getting an inferior product."

Many transcribers still enter all their braille by hand even when they are using a computer, she explained. Slower than regular typing, entering braille by hand is called "six-key" entry because the first three fingers of each hand enter the six braille dots. "I use software that translates," she explains, "and then after it's turned to braille I fix what it doesn't do right before it gets printed [embossed].

"What I like best about braille transcription is the opportunity to contribute to someone's education by providing a quality product," she says. "It makes me feel good when we get good feedback from blind students who formerly struggled through math courses with inaccurate transcriptions."

If you already know MS Word or WordPerfect, you're in a good position to start learning braille software. However, software makes mistakes when it comes to judgments about such things as the style of a paragraph. A person who doesn't understand the concepts behind braille writing may make serious errors.

Transcribers may be certified at several levels, including literary, Nemeth, and music, among others. All certified transcribers must first pass literary certification, and have completed either a correspondence course or classes through a community college to gain the skills for passing the course. For this level of certification, they learn the braille code, the rules (such as when to use abbreviations), and layouts of paragraphs and pages. For the final test, the student submits a sample 50-page manuscript. Learning braille may take 18 months in a correspondence course, but may go faster at a local community college or a volunteer group.

Many school districts and public agencies hire one certified transcriber and a group of noncertified individuals who work with the certified person. The non-certified transcriber relies on software to make sure that they're following rules for proper transcription.

Most braille transcribers work from home or in small offices. If you work for yourself, you'll need to build a network of referrals among other transcribers. There are also lists of transcribers posted with many Web sites, such as the Duxbury Systems Web site at http://www.duxsys.com or the American Printing House for the Blind at http://www.aph.org. If you'd rather have a larger employer safety net, you can look for a job at a major institution, such as school districts or universities.

Pitfalls

There's no doubt that the job can be tedious. Braille transcription is a slow, methodical chore, so unless you've got someone reading over your shoulder, you must read each word and compare it to the print text. Looking between the computer screen and the hard copy hour after hour becomes very tiring, especially after the second or third time. There are some concerns that the number of jobs will decrease since only about 10 percent of blind Americans use braille consistently. The rest use other formats, such as large print or audio books. If you work independently, you'll also have to buy your own equipment, which come in varying sizes, speeds and costs. Machines start at about $1,500 for 15 characters per second (cps), hit 50 cps at $4,000, then follow that trend of $100 per additional cps.

Perks

Braille transcribing is an attractive job for people who prefer to work in solitary environments and who relish very methodical, detailed work. Knowing that you're helping blind individuals have access to all kinds of material is also a very satisfying feeling.

Get a Jump on the Job

Practice your typing and editing skills at school, and learn MS Word, which is an important basis from which to learn braille transcription. Read all you can about braille and transcription. Check out the National Braille Association Web site and see if you can find someone locally to talk to about learning braille, or check out the California Transcribers and Educators of the Visually Handicapped (see Appendix A for contact information).

There are also opportunities to work for local school districts and other organizations while learning to transcribe.

BROADCAST CAPTIONER

OVERVIEW

You probably don't pay much attention to those real-time captions at the bottom of the screen during live TV programs such as news shows. But they don't get there by accident—they are provided by broadcast captioners, captioning 30 to 40 hours of programs a week. That doesn't include time spent preparing to make sure their software and equipment are ready to handle the content of a broadcast.

This is a job that appeals to the freelancing spirit, since you don't have to work in an office to caption—you can operate right in your own home, as long as you have the right kind of computer equipment.

Captions are visual depictions of the soundtrack of a video program or film. Unlike subtitles, which simply translate the dialogue, captions also include song lyrics and descriptions of sound effects. They may also indicate who is speaking and may include special vocal inflection. Although captioning was originally developed for people who were deaf or hard of hearing, today captions help people learn English as a second language. They also help those watching TV in public places such as a bar, where viewers may not be able to hear the TV. Captioning of most broadcast and cablecast programming was mandated under the Telecommunications Act of 1996.

Real-time captioners provide captions for the live portion of a broadcast and are usually first trained as court reporters. Typically, captioning companies provide

AT A GLANCE

Salary Range

At an average of $50 to $100 for every programming hour, top captioners might earn between $60,000 and $120,000 a year, with benefits. Captioners earn a wide range of fees per program hour, depending on the type of program being captioned, experience, and the company for whom the person is working.

Education/Experience

Aspiring broadcast captioners will need at least three years of full-time education, unless they're already court reporters, in which case they might need a year of retraining. To be trained as a court reporter, a student should attend a school accredited by the National Court Reporters Association. Most offer associate degree and certificate programs.

Personal Attributes

Broadcast captioners usually enjoy working alone, and must be able to work under stress. Their work must be flawless, because viewers are depending on the text to be accurate. They must be intelligent and have the ability to concentrate and significant physical stamina to provide real-time captions for many hours of live television.

Requirements

If you're an independent contractor, you'll need the proper computer equipment in order to work from home. You'll also need to be able to produce 200 to 225 words per minute, which is the typical graduation requirement for court reporters. There are no certification requirements, but many firms are impressed by membership in the National Court Reporters Association, which awards certifications including Certified Realtime Reporter and Certified Broadcast Captioner. Captioners should have no more than three errors per file page (including punctuation).

Outlook

Excellent. This is a growing field, with skilled captioners in high demand.

Kathy DiLorenzo, former real-time captioner

A career as a real-time broadcast captioner was the farthest thing from Kathy DiLorenzo's mind when she was in high school. In her senior year, her strong shorthand and typing skills brought her to the attention of her business teachers. "I was a very fast typist," she recalls, "and I went to typing competitions, where I would win handily." As a result, her teachers suggested she apply for a full scholarship to attend secretarial school. Once she applied, she found out about the career of court reporting, and won a scholarship to study in that area.

She had worked as a court reporter for five years when she found out about the career of real-time captioning in 1986—and she never looked back. She's spent the years since as an employee of Vitac, a company that employs both court reporters and captioners all over the country; today, she's vice president of national reporter relations.

When she first started, she captioned *World News Tonight with Peter Jennings* and *Good Morning America*. "It's extremely intense," she says, "listening to every word being said and writing it on a machine that's phonetically based. Every stroke must match on a computer translation of a word, and you're hoping it's the right word. That all comes with skill level."

So when you're captioning live, in real time, what happens when you get behind?

"That's the difference between being a captioner and a court reporter," she says. "A court reporter is responsible for making a record of what's being said, so they can interrupt the proceedings, ask someone to speak more slowly. As a captioner, I couldn't pick up the phone and call Peter Jennings and say: 'Slow down!' You need to have the ability to edit when you get behind, to summarize. You do the best you can to make the content readable and understandable to the viewer. The easiest way to do the job is to be very fast—a quick thinker and a quick writer—so you can process information very quickly so you're not called upon to edit. It's much easier to write everything that's being said than it is to synopsize. Your goal is always to be 100 percent accurate verbatim."

Despite the intensity and the pressure, DiLorenzo truly loved real time captioning. "Most captioners love writing on their machines," she says. "Other than the actual writing part, I enjoyed working to get my skills to where they needed to be. I was involved in news, I loved hearing the news and being up on all types of world politics, news stories, and entertainment news—anything that was news. Real-time captioners are probably the best conversational people you'll meet."

The key to successful captioning news, she says, is to know exactly what's going on in the world so you're prepared to know how to spell all those unusual foreign names of leaders and countries. "You need a broad range of knowledge in media, and you have to know it like the back of your hand. You have to recognize a name when you hear it, know how write it phonetically."

complete captioning services to a wide variety of producers, broadcasters, webcasters, and syndicators in the entertainment, governmental, and educational fields. These companies also provide multi-language subtitling services, video description, and V-chip encoding services. Captioning is a highly specialized end of the court reporting field and demands the best of skills—speed, accuracy, and a broad range of knowledge in all television-related areas.

Most broadcast captioners use a steno machine (or steno writer) with 24 keys and a number bar. When the captioner depresses the keys, it produces letters on a computer screen or paper tape. Study of

Of course, no job is perfect, and for DiLorenzo, the hours could be difficult. Back when she was first captioning, everyone had to work out of the company's headquarters in either Washington, D.C., Boston, or in Pittsburgh. "TV is on 24-7, and I had to be in the office by 4 a.m. I'm a morning person, though, and I kind of hold that same schedule today. At that time we worked in eight- or 10-hour shifts. You may only have been captioning for two hours; the rest of the time you spent training to get very very good."

Captioners don't have that luxury anymore, she explains, since 90 percent of real-time captioners work from their homes. "Modern technology allows us to do that," she says. "Instead of shift work now, you'll work from 4 a.m. to noon, or 6 a.m. to 2 p.m. Today, captioners work whatever programming they want or hours they want, and so they may do two hours in the early morning, then work again from 11 a.m. to noon, then pick up a game in the evening. They are able to caption far more hours a day, because they can pick up hours all over the clock."

Practice time is fitted in between the captioning gigs. "As you get more experience, the less you have to practice," she says. "A very experienced captioner will look on Web sites to get the most recent news stories, and their prep time will involve adding entries for words they may not have in their dictionaries."

Like all captioners, DiLorenzo's early training was in court reporting, and she enjoys both careers. "They both offer very unique and lucrative opportunities for both women and men. It's a professional field and the better you perform on your own, the better you do in this field. Your success in the field isn't depending on someone else saying you're successful—it's what you prove it to be."

No matter which field you choose—broadcast captioning or court reporting—DiLorenzo says you'll never have a boring day. "There's always something new and every day is wonderful. It's an extremely rewarding, flexible, and lucrative career."

If this sounds good to you, she recommends you spend time in school perfecting your typing—but success as a captioner is only partly based on typing skill. "Folks who thrive in this profession are people who are very into words, the English language, who can process information quickly, who are well-read, who can hear a word and instantly know how it's spelled. I've questioned over the years whether digital agility helps that much. It's more a grasp of the English language. If you're in love with the English language and the media, you'd love this field."

the basic theory takes time and determination, and learning how to do broadcast captions takes much practice. Broadcast captioners must be able to type as close to word-for-word as possible, but because captioners can't stop the speaker to catch up, captioners must be able to edit the text as required. They must find the best way to get readable text to the screen, which may require condensing the content while keeping the meaning clear.

Even if you're working at the lightning-fast speed of 225 words per minute (wpm), you can't just turn the television on and expect to be able to caption the news. That's a type of captioning that can be very difficult and takes a great deal of time and practice to master. Captioners practice with literary material on tape, or taped lectures. It's most important to understand what you're writing. The more you know or the more that you learn, the better broadcast captioner you'll be. You must know both the meaning and the spelling of the word. To tackle captioning the news, you want to be sure that you understand the content before you start to write it. Most captioners read the paper every day, entering names and words into the caption dictionary. That way, when you sit down to write the news, it may seem fast but the terminology won't sound foreign. Your goal as a captioner is always 100 percent accuracy. When you apply for a captioning position, your writing will be closely evaluated for content and for accuracy. You'll get the job only if you can produce accurate translation as near to verbatim as possible.

Pitfalls

If you work independently out of your home, you'll probably need to invest about $18,000 to get the right computers and software. The job can be quite stressful, as you must pay incredibly close attention to what's happening and what's being said in order to caption correctly.

Perks

This is a very high-paying job that can be very satisfying to someone who enjoys the challenge of captioning live events. The ability to work at home is also of great appeal.

Get a Jump on the Job

Practice captioning in 15-minute segments by listening to a tape. When you've completed the 15-minute practice, go back and review your file word for word to catch errors. Figure out why the errors occurred—a misstroke, an improperly written word, or a misheard word. Then write the same segment many times, if necessary, with an eye toward perfecting your writing and learning from the errors that you made.

BUTLER

OVERVIEW

In 19th-century Britain, the butler was the snobbish king of everything that went on below stairs, but the title originally applied to the person in charge of the wine cellar, derived from the old French *bouteillier* ("bottle bearer"). In time, the word *butler* came to mean "an official of the crown"—a person of high rank who was in charge of the wine. Eventually, the butler's duties expanded as his aristocratic rank dropped.

Being a modern butler today is very much a managerial executive position. Most butlers work for private, extremely wealthy people (although some work with luxury hotels or corporations). The International Guild of Professional Butlers estimates that there are about 50,000 professional butlers manning entrances, buffing silver, and managing households throughout the world.

The butler is the chief servant of the household and he or she supervises other employees, receives guests, oversees meal service, and performs a host of other personal services. As the butler of a home, you'll be responsible for the rest of the staff, the yacht, the jet, and all the other properties owned by the family. If you're a woman, that doesn't mean you can't be a butler. The International Guild of Professional Butlers reports that many families employ female butlers; families in the Middle and Far East often prefer female butlers, as do a lot of female celebrities.

A butler's main job is to oversee the household staff, which often means riding herd on employees at more than one residence, organizing their duties and schedules, hiring, training, and firing. Strictly speaking, the butler isn't responsible for the gardener or chauffeur, but today most butlers do oversee these positions as well.

Entertaining is another big part of the job. Butlers are expected to organize parties and events. Understanding etiquette and protocol is vital, since the butler receives guests and supervises receptions, and may prepare the guest room with flowers, towels, fruit, or drinks. Classically the butler cares for the silver and glassware and is responsible for every small detail in the house from the wine cellar to the attics. Butlers also may be asked to double as house manager, personal assistant, valet, chef, or bodyguard.

But it doesn't stop there. Butlers are also expected to schedule and oversee household maintenance and care of stables, boats, and planes, while performing light housekeeping duties. Butlers may act as a sort of concierge, too, booking hotels, restaurants, and theater seats. Household accounting and creating household budgets is yet another task, as is dealing with contractors or workers and supervising their tasks.

Charles MacPherson, former butler

Becoming a butler was never a vocation that Charles MacPherson dreamt about. "It was just one I fell into," he says. After graduating from a Toronto college with an honors diploma in hotel management and completing an internship program at the Cornell School of Hospitality, he worked in the restaurant business before establishing his own catering company, Babette's Feast, which he operated for five years. A native of Toronto, Charles has also lived in Paris and is fluent in English and French.

He was busily running Babette's Feast when one of his clients—one of Canada's most prominent families—asked him to sell his catering business to become a butler for them. "It was the most incredible experience of my life," he says. "I wasn't aware that such jobs existed."

He spent the next five years managing three households, an island, the dogs, and the kids— "the whole kit and caboodle," he says. "I must sum up that experience and say truly, absolutely, it was the best time of my life. I was exposed to things that I've only thought were in fantasyland. I didn't know such luxuries existed. Truly, you didn't realize there really is a very private world. And the secret for me was that the family I worked for was so kind and generous, they made me want to work hard and harder for them."

What bothered him the most about being a butler was a personal fear of disappointing. "I always wanted to make the family and their guests happy," he says. "The fear of disappointing the family was great." He also was unhappy about the fact that he wasn't strong enough as a person to take more time off for himself—"so I worked too much, and I didn't smell the roses. Being a workaholic, I still haven't learned."

After five years of butling, the family's kids were all going off to universities, the family was downsizing, "and I decided my fear was to get the golden handshake," he says. "I couldn't justify why they needed an expensive toy like myself." As a result, MacPherson came up with the idea of doing for many different families what he had been doing for just one—and Charles MacPherson Associates was born. His residential management firm oversees estates and is dedicated to the development and implementation of custom solutions to help operate properties in a professional, efficient, and cost-effective manner. "I don't really believe anyone likes a job 100 percent," he says, "but I truly loved my job [as a butler]."

There's still more. Many butlers double as a personal assistant, maintaining the wardrobe and clothing inventory for the gentleman of the house, including packing and preparing for travel, as well as handling correspondence, keeping the calendar, and taking care of various other secretarial duties.

It's not an easy task to manage a 21st-century household. In addition to all the above tasks, butlers also need to know styles of service, table manners, wines and champagnes, cigars, special celebrations, laundry (including linens and fine fabric care), clothing maintenance, ironing and pressing, dry cleaning, dress codes, formal wear, buying clothing and shoes, maintaining inventories, and packing suitcases. Butlers must also know how to address people of different cultures and titled persons (including royalty).

Pitfalls

Butling is hard work, just like any other job. When working for a private family, the butler usually lives in an apartment in the main house, or in a house on the estate, which can be difficult since the butler never really leaves the job. In addition, a butler is on call 24 hours a day, which makes it tough to do this job if you have a family. If you have to move abroad or change residences, your kids would have to change schools. Pets might be difficult to keep as well. And even if your family isn't employed directly by your boss, they must behave and dress as if they were.

Perks

You'll have a great salary, free room and board, and free clothing, along with the ability to travel around the world. The job can be challenging but also highly satisfying, and can reveal a luxurious way of life you may never have realized.

Get a Jump on the Job

Since butlers must be experienced in food, service, household management, and staff management, anything you can do to get experience in any of these areas would be helpful. Working after school, on weekends, or during the summer in restaurants or hotels would offer you lots of experience. In college, you might consider majoring in hotel management or business.

CAREER COUNSELOR

OVERVIEW

For some people, the perfect job is helping other people to find their perfect job. Career counselors work with people of all ages, from students still in high school to individuals in their 40s, 50s, and beyond. And they help people in all walks of life, from high school dropouts to people with advanced university degrees, who for one reason or another need their services.

An individual's first contact with a career counselor probably takes place in high school, where the job is often called "school counselor." Long before a student is ready to make a career decision, the counselor will use an assortment of tools and assessments to help get an idea of the student's interests and skills. Based on the results of those assessments, the counselor will work with the student to investigate careers that best fit those results. The counselor will also help the student select a class schedule.

As students get closer to graduation, the role of the counselor begins to change. Counselors will continue to evaluate abilities, interests, talents, and personalities to help students determine career opportunities. For college-bound students, they will help select the most appropriate college for the individual's goals and needs. Counselors may help students through the admissions process and even assist them in locating financial aid. For students choosing to enter the work world right out of high school, counselors will help with practical job search skills like preparing a resume and interviewing skills.

AT A GLANCE

Salary Range

The median annual salary for individuals working as career counselors was just about $44,000, with half earning between $33,000 and nearly $57,000.

Education/Experience

Most positions will require at least a bachelor's degree. Many career counselors have experience in vocational work and some also have degrees or experience in social work.

Personal Attributes

Career counselors need to have a genuine desire to help people. They need to have excellent listening and communication skills. Career counselors need to be nonjudgmental, patient, and able to inspire trust and confidence in their clients. Good teaching skills are also helpful.

Requirements

Requirements vary from state to state based on the specialty in which the individual is working. Individuals working in a school setting are required in all 50 states to have a state school counseling certificate as well as some graduate coursework, with many requiring a completed master's degree. Some states will also require school counselors to have a teaching certificate. In 47 states as well as the District of Columbia, counselors working outside a school setting are required to have some sort of credentials, licensure, or certification. Requirements to meet those credentials may include a master's degree, supervised clinical experience, passage of an exam, continuing education, and more. Career counselors working in private practice may need to file Doing Business As (DBA) papers and acquire any other permits required under local and/or state ordinances.

Outlook

Jobs for career counselors are expected to grow as more individuals hoping to make informed career decisions become aware of their services. With a

(continues)

College career counselors perform many of the same tasks as high school counselors. They will help students undecided on a major to investigate career possibilities based on the student's interests, abilities, and personality traits. The college counselor probably won't suggest classes for the student to take, instead referring him to an advisor in the specific academic department in which he's considering studying.

Career counselors can also be of help to students who have decided on a specific major. College career centers often have information centers with information on many different jobs, and what career options a student might have if he studies a particular field. For example, a student who has decided she wants to study math could investigate the job possibilities open to her, such as teaching, statistics, or actuarial science.

As students prepare to graduate and make the transition from college to the working world, career counselors will once again be an invaluable resource. Counselors help students develop and polish the skills they need to get that first career job, through a variety of workshops covering things like preparing a resume, writing a cover letter, and dressing for success. They work with students in mock interviews, teaching the dos and don'ts of proper interviewing. Counselors at smaller schools may even assist students in networking with alumni working in the same field. Colleges and universities often offer the services of their career counselors to alumni as well.

Many people are familiar with the work of career counselors in high schools and colleges or universities, but what they might not know is that career counselors work with individuals well beyond the high school and college years. These counselors may be employed by a public or government agency, some work for private employment agencies, and others are independent career counselors in private practice.

People turn to these career counselors for help for any number of reasons. A person facing a layoff after many years in the same job might need help in planning for a new career. A mother who took time off to raise children may need advice on reentering the workforce, or maybe entering it for the first time. A high school dropout living on welfare may be ordered to find and keep a full-time job. Or, maybe a successful business executive is miserable at a job he's hated for many years, and is looking for a new and fulfilling career. Career counselors can help all these people.

Many career counselors will use the same sorts of tools and assessments with these individuals to determine their interests, skills, abilities, values, preferences, personality traits, strengths and weaknesses, previous work history and experience, and more. The counselor will often have to take into account where the person is at in his or her life, and what he or she has experienced. For example, if an individual can't read, the counselor will track down the services needed to overcome that problem.

Career counselors don't actually find jobs for their clients, but they work to give

Deb Schafer, job search instructor

I have never been so happy in a job. My husband says I even come home [from work] happy. I get to see people succeed," says Deb Schafer, a job search instructor for a state employment agency. For many of Schafer's clients, even small successes are often major accomplishments. "I am so excited to see those successes. There is no other job where you can see that."

In the state where Schafer works, welfare recipients are required to spend 40 hours a week in job training and preparation classes. They will stay in the classroom with Schafer until they're ready to start their job search; at that point, they'll spend two hours each day out in the community looking for a job.

Schafer's clients don't usually come to her under the best of circumstances. Schafer says her background in sociology with a concentration in criminal justice has helped prepare her for this job. After college, she spent five years as an intensive in-home social worker working with kids in neglectful or abusive situations. Her experiences have helped her understand the type of homes and situations in which her clients grew up.

"When they come to me, they are already torn down," she says. "I can't judge them, I have to take them where they are at and go from there." It's not unusual for Schafer to see people over and over again in her classes. "I give them a fresh start every time [they come back]. It may take multiple times to find the right job."

In her classes, Schafer teaches all the skills her students need to prepare for, find, maintain, and succeed at a job. She teaches students how to prepare a resume, write a cover letter and thank-you notes, and how to participate in an interview. Some of the skills she teaches involve things that many people take for granted, such as how to get your clothes ready for an interview, or how to mend, hem, and iron. Schafer even takes her clients shopping at area thrift and resale shops to help them find interview-appropriate clothing. She teaches her female students how to apply makeup, and if necessary, she works with them on personal hygiene issues. She'll also teach social skills and even how to set goals.

But getting a job and keeping a job require two different sets of skills. Schafer also works with her clients on how to keep a job, and includes courses in stress relief and personal care. She also addresses anger management, harassment, and sensitivity in the workplace. In addition, Schafer brings different speakers into her classroom to cover topics such as nutrition, how to establish and live within a budget, making the transition away from food stamps, as well as the transition from Medicaid to private insurance.

Yet as much as Schafer loves her job, at times it can be very stressful. "You have to be vigilant about not getting jaded and burned out," she warns. "Every person deserves a chance, but when you burn out, you can't help anyone. You have to take care of yourself and keep your emotions in check." In fact, Schafer's boss encourages her employees to take a "mental health" day when she sees that they are burning out.

As for Schafer, who has deep religious convictions, she says, "I get to help people every day. For me, it's mission work. I can't talk about my faith, but it shows. You aren't going to make a lot of money, but you definitely get your rewards in other ways."

the clients all the skills they need to make that career change and then be successful in that new career.

If you are interested in becoming an expert on all sorts of different careers and the resources needed to get and keep a job, and you like working with and helping people, career counseling might be the perfect fit for you.

Pitfalls

The pitfalls vary from job to job. In some situations, career counselors see and work with people who have hit rock bottom, which can become somewhat depressing. Some career counselors burn out over time, and need to make a career change of their own. Sometimes, career counselors are faced with pressure from their supervisors to place students or clients into any position, even if it isn't a good fit for the individual, to improve their numbers.

Perks

Career counselors get the opportunity to meet a diverse range of people and work with those people to find the profession that best fits their skills, needs, and abilities. For many people, having the opportunity to work in a job they enjoy can mean less stressful, happier, more productive lives. For others, it is truly life changing.

Get a Jump on the Job

Since a college or university degree, and often an advanced degree, is almost always required to work as a career counselor, focus on those classes that are required to get into a school that can help you reach your goals. Your career counselor can help you research schools and advise you on what classes to take.

ETIQUETTE CONSULTANT

OVERVIEW

Do you eat asparagus with a fork or your fingers? Can you pick up a chicken leg with your hands and nibble it in public? Is it okay to e-mail a thank-you note?

You're not born knowing which spoon to use, how to set a table, and how to address a bishop—you learn those skills. And because good manners are vital not only in a social sense, but also if you want to advance in the corporate world, there are plenty of opportunities for manners consultants to earn a living as a specialist. This might include corporate etiquette, children's or teen etiquette, tea party etiquette, entertaining etiquette, dining etiquette, international protocol, and social or wedding etiquette.

Most etiquette consultants own their own businesses and make a very good living teaching other people how to handle themselves in a variety of situations. Typically, lessons may include how to meet and greet a variety of individuals (including corporate higher-ups, potential interviewers, royalty, religious leaders, well-known politicians, celebrities, and more). Lessons also may include party manners, appropriate dress, hosting duties, manners in public places, restaurant dining skills, telephone and cell phone manners, social skills, thank you notes, behavior at religious services and events, international protocol, and wedding details.

As an etiquette consultant, you can teach people the skills they need to succeed in business and in life.

AT A GLANCE

Salary Range

Your salary depends on exactly what type of consulting you do and whether you own your own etiquette business, but many consultants earn thousands of dollars a day by presenting corporate seminars and workshops in this field.

Education/Experience

No special education or experience is necessary, but a solid understanding of etiquette and protocol is important.

Personal Attributes

Excellent manners, attention to detail, politeness, plus an ability to work well with others.

Requirements

A thorough knowledge of manners and etiquette.

Outlook

Becoming an etiquette consultant is a growing field as both businesses and schools are reaching out for help in teaching manners to workers and students.

You can specialize in coaching adults or children on proper etiquette. For example, with your help, the sloppy eater who used to shovel in his food and burp at the table can be transformed into a charming dining companion whom everyone wants to invite to dinner.

Many etiquette consultants are hired by private clients, but you might also be hired by corporations to help young managers learn proper business etiquette or teach a senior executive how to make a good impression meeting with clients from different countries. Or you might teach telephone etiquette to customer service staff.

Jodi R. R. Smith, manners consultant

Jodi Smith likes to point out that she's neither a blue-blooded Brahmin nor a debutante—and she never even attended finishing school. But ever since she watched the "popular kids" in high school, Smith has been fascinated with why people behave as they do and why some people have better social skills than others.

Armed with a degree in motivational psychology and a master's in labor relations, Smith has worked with organizations, corporations, educational institutions, and individuals to increase their social savvy and confidence levels. Her experience in corporate human resources has bolstered her belief that proper manners and etiquette are an important part of success in today's world.

"I spent a decade in human resources, and I found that there were lots of really smart people who weren't as successful as they should have been because they lacked social skills," she explains. "In the companies I worked for, I started to give many presentations on etiquette to anybody who wanted to sign up." Then she moved into more formalized seminars for entire departments, managers, and so on. "They really need the information to succeed," she explains.

That's when the phone calls from friends and neighbors started. "I got phone calls and e-mails from people I worked with two jobs ago, saying: 'My husband, neighbor, sister . . . is looking for a new job and can you talk to them about etiquette?' I started spending so much time doing that, on nights and weekends, that my husband jokingly said: 'You should start a business!'"

Today—10 years later—her company (Mannersmith) has grown by leaps and bounds. This etiquette consulting firm creates and delivers seminars to clients ranging from children to CEOs, providing "tips, techniques, strategies, and ideas" that her clients can use to better handle themselves in social and work situations. Each program is a combination of lecture, activities, and exercises that are designed to ensure that learning about manners is both educational and entertaining.

Smith tailors all her workshops and seminars to fit the age, interest level, and size of any group. Through her company, she offers a range of popular programs, including a "gracious dining" seminar and a "small talk and conversation" seminar. She also offers bar/bat mitzvah etiquette programs, "dating today" for people interested in meeting new people and building relationships, and a "wedding preparations" seminar. Her business protocol seminars are designed for business executives who need to improve their social savvy. Networking and interviewing seminars can help people advance in their career, prepare for an interview, or build their business. She also focuses on college with an "interview and application" seminar designed for high school juniors and seniors as they prepare for university admissions, and a "campus to career" seminar for students about to graduate from college or complete a graduate program.

"I love what I do," she says. "It's fun! And it's important for anybody, whatever job they're doing, that they should choose what they enjoy. This stuff isn't rocket science, so when I give a seminar or somebody reads one of my books, they get it—there's not a whole long learning curve. They can hear the information and immediately put it to use."

If you ask most people what etiquette is, she says, they'll tell you it's about knowing what fork to use, and that's part of it. "But what etiquette is really about is using behaviors so that you are comfortable with yourself and able to make those around you feel comfortable," she explains.

(continues)

(continued)

"Taking into account comfort and consideration as primary elements in etiquette, my background makes perfect sense."

That doesn't mean that everything about her career has been one long easy romp through the woods. "It's not easy to be an entrepreneur," she cautions. "When people tell me they want to start their own business, I tell them they have to love what they do, because it's a lot of work. You're everything—you're the secretary, the copy guy, the IT department. You really need to like what you're doing."

If you think that owning your own manners consulting business sounds like fun, Smith suggests that you should take as many psychology and sociology courses as you can to better understand some of the theories behind interpersonal reactions. It's also a good idea to find a company and intern or apprentice with them

What she likes best, she says, is that she really helps people live better lives. "I find that very satisfying," she says. "I get a lot of e-mails and phone calls from participants to tell me they've taken the ideas and used them and it's made their life better."

Pitfalls

Most manners consultants own their own businesses, which means that all of the responsibility of the business—and stress—fall on your shoulders. If you don't work, you don't eat, and if you take a vacation or sick day, you don't get paid. You'll need to be an expert in keeping track of taxes, handling insurance, and more.

Perks

If you love working with people and you're an outgoing sort, it can be enormous fun to help others learn how to be more effec-tive in their personal and business lives. The ability to earn an excellent income is almost unlimited if you're good at presenting seminars and workshops for the corporate world.

Get a Jump on the Job

The earlier you learn about manners, the better—but if the whole field of etiquette fascinates you, try to read as much as you can about the proper way to handle every situation. Take some etiquette courses yourself, and read about protocol.

FITTING MODEL

OVERVIEW

The term "fit model" may conjure up the image of a beautiful person on the cover of *Shape* magazine—but fit (or "fitting") models actually have very little to do with the exercise industry. In fact, fitting models usually aren't seen by more than a couple of people, because their job is to stand there perfectly still while a garment is being constructed on their body. The fitting model may model outfits in a manufacturer's showroom and let the designers, clothes makers, and buyers know what works and what doesn't about an outfit, such as how the material falls and how it feels. A fitting model's job is vital because creating garments that are fit only on a form (or directly from a pattern) doesn't let the designer allow for natural variances, and this often results in a less desirable fit. Fitting models are real people chosen for the job based on their average body type, proportion, and their measurements that best meet specifications for their size. Fitting models can include just about everybody—women and men, boys and girls, toddlers and infants—and this type of modeling doesn't usually involve print work or advertising photo sessions. Instead, they just stand in a designer's studio for hours while clothes are created on their bodies.

If you've got a perfect size and your dimensions match fashion industry standards (including "plus," "petite," and "big and tall" sizes), you may find you're in demand for work with a clothing company or clothes designer. The most successful fitting models—the ones who make six figures—know how clothes are made, know

AT A GLANCE

Salary Range

A successful fit model can earn between $750 and $1,500 a day; on an hourly basis, that might be between $175 and $300 (but modeling agencies take a 15 percent commission). Fitting models typically work three to five days a week, for between five and eight hours a day. Annual salaries for successful models may range from $100,000 to $300,000 a year.

Education/Experience

No specific education is required, but a solid understanding of materials, fabrics, and clothing is helpful.

Personal Attributes

Patience, stamina, a flexible attitude, and a professional manner are important, as is the ability to maintain a consistent body size.

Requirements

Fit modeling requires consistent measurements based on specifications for that size, including the correct height, torso, arm length, leg length, bust, waist, and hips, along with all other body measurements. These measurements must be maintained to within a half inch. You must also have good posture and the ability to stand on your feet for hours at a time. It's also helpful to know a lot about clothing and how things should feel and move with the body, since designers often rely on fitting models' feedback in order to perfect a design. Because fitting is a "hands on" business, you must be comfortable with your clothing being handled, pinned, marked, cut, or otherwise adjusted on you.

Outlook

Good. Clothing manufacturers continue to need a supply of fitting models to help them perfect the designs for their clothing.

how different fabrics behave, and understand the line they're modeling. In fact, many have degrees in pattern making.

Erica Hartse, fit model

Ever since she was small, Erica Hartse, now 13, wanted to model and be an actress. The 5'6" fit model has worked for Target, for girls size 8 and juniors size 1. She got started in the business at age 7, when her mom saw an ad in their local Minneapolis paper looking for fit models. "Target said I was a perfect fit model," Erica explains, because of her body type. "I really liked it—they gave me free clothes. And the people were also really nice." She also really liked most of the clothes she modeled. The only downside, she says, was that sometimes she got poked with pins.

If fit modeling sounds like something you'd enjoy doing, Erica suggests that you need to be patient and to follow the rules: no gum chewing, no food or water, no siblings in the room, and be on time! You also have to be careful to maintain your weight and your measurements.

In addition to her fit modeling, Hartse also works as an actress, a runway model, and a stunt double. In fact, the family left Minneapolis and now lives in California, where the call for fit modeling is less. "There's not so many places that need fit models out here," she says. Instead, Erica has begun mannequin modeling—a job for which she says fit modeling prepared her very well.

When she's not fit modeling or acting, Erica also loves rock climbing, parasailing, fencing, dirt biking, electric guitar, singing, dancing, swimming, horseback riding, snowboarding, ice skating, rollerblading, and biking.

You can watch for Erica in the movie *Shredder Man* and in *Zoey 101* on Nickelodeon.

While you don't need the face of a goddess, you have to be attractive and be able to project a certain image. The hardest part of being a fitting model is maintaining the same size at all times. This means no gorging on double cheeseburgers and gaining three inches around the waist, which could spell disaster for your career. If you went on a job last week with a 24-inch waist, your waist had better be the same size when you go back this week. Although small variances are allowed as slight natural fluctuations in measurements are realistic, a significant gain can spell trouble, because if somebody else more closely meets the company's size requirements, the client may decide to replace you.

Unlike other types of models, if you're interested in a career as a fitting model, you won't need any up-front costs—no headshots or composite cards, no portfolio—and you won't even need any modeling or fitting experience (although for some jobs, experienced fit models may be preferred).

If you're a well-proportioned individual of average height with consistent measurements, you're just what the company might be looking for. In fact, being an "average fit" is better than having a "runway" or "athletic" look. Think girl or boy next door.

Although sizing and fit specifications vary by client and clothing line, you can expect that clothing would be fit on "core" sizes (those in the middle of a particular size range). Fit models in other sizes may be booked to offer a comparison fit to the core size, however. Typical core sizes include:

- "Women": 10, 18W, 20W
- "Men": 40 Reg, 44 Reg, 48 Reg
- "Juniors" (must be 18 years or older): 9, 19, 21
- "Boys": 5, 6, 8

- "Girls": 5, 6, 8, 12
- "Toddlers": 3T (boys or girls; no diapers)
- "Infants": girls or boys 18 months of age.

Fit models are booked for individual fit sessions of one or two hours or more, often with short advance notice, based on the clothing requirements. Some sizes fit weekly, with models booked either in advance or as needed, but other fitting models are booked on a regular, recurring schedule.

Pitfalls

As a fitting model, you'll generally make less money than other types of models, where the sky's the limit.

Perks

Although you may not earn as much as other models, you'll be much more likely to work more steadily, for longer days, and you can still earn a six-figure income if you're good and you work hard. There is typically less pressure in this type of modeling than for runway modeling in which your face is your fortune, and any minor blemish can spell disaster.

Get a Jump on the Job

Try to read as much as you can about this job, and talk to people in the field. See if you can get a part-time or summer job with a clothing or design firm and watch how the fitting models work.

FORTUNE COOKIE WRITER

OVERVIEW

There it sits on your plate, a shiny brown little confection filled with crunchy sweetness—and a little slip of paper with a fortune and a lucky number. For almost 100 years, Chinese food aficionados have enjoyed fishing into their dessert cookie to find the pithy little statements at the end of their meal.

But who writes the fortunes, and how did it all get started? Some historians have suggested that the idea behind fortune cookies originated in the 14th century, when Chinese soldiers slipped messages into moon cakes as they planned their overthrow of Mongolian invaders, but in fact, fortune cookies have never been a part of Chinese food culture. Fortune cookies are almost unknown in China—they're strictly an American invention, although precisely where it all started is mired in controversy.

Both San Francisco and Los Angeles insist they are the birthplace of the fortune cookie. Some say Makoto Hagiwara of Golden Gate Park's Japanese Tea Garden in San Francisco invented the cookie in 1909, while others swear that Canton-born David Jung, founder of the Hong Kong Noodle Company in Los Angeles, invented them in 1918. Things got so heated that the whole matter was taken to San Francisco's Court of Historical Review, which ruled in 1983 in favor of San Francisco. (However, while a federal judge presided over the court, the hear-

ing itself has been criticized as being biased in favor of San Francisco.)

In any case, it's clear that the cookie was invented somewhere in California at the turn of the century. Fortune cookies are served as snacks after meals at most North American Chinese restaurants, where diners eat the cookie first and then read the fortune.

Indeed, they are served almost exclusively in North American Chinese restaurants, where they are referred to as "genuine American fortune cookies." Dessert at a true Chinese restaurant

Donald Lau, fortune cookie writer

As a vice president at Wonton Food, Inc., in Long Island City, New York, Donald Lau juggles a lot of career balls, including managing the company's accounts payable and receivable, negotiating with suppliers, and composing the fortunes that go inside his company's fortune cookies. Wonton is the world's largest manufacturer of the tiny confections, churning out four million Golden Bowl-brand cookies every single day. These are sold to several hundred venders, who, in turn, sell them to most of the 40,000 Chinese restaurants across the United States.

Lau didn't start out in life intending to become a fortune-cookie writer. After graduating from Columbia University with degrees in engineering and business, he joined Bank of America, and then ran a company exporting logs from the Pacific Northwest to China. In the early eighties, he was hired by a Chinatown noodle manufacturer, which eventually expanded into fortune cookies. When the firm bought the Long Island City plant, it became obvious that the company's old-fashioned catalogue of fortunes from the 1940s needed to be updated.

"We knew we needed to add new sayings," Lau says. "I was chosen because my English was the best of the group, not because I'm a poet," he explained in an interview with the *New Yorker*. The writing came easily to him at first, and Lau searched for inspiration all over the place, from the *I Ching* to the daily newspaper. Every day, Lau cranked out three or four pithy sayings between crunching numbers and monitoring the company's noodle inventory. On his way to work, he'd check out the subway signs, jotting down fortune ideas in a small notebook. He never sat in front of a flickering computer screen and told himself he had to write 15 fortunes. Instead, he thought the ideas needed to flow naturally.

Eventually, however, there's a limit to the punchy little philosophic ideas that can be contained in just one sentence, and after about 11 years Lau's fortune fount began to run dry. He began to pilfer more and more from traditional Chinese sayings, until in 1995 he gave up altogether, abandoning the job to a permanent case of writer's block. "I've written thousands of fortunes, but the inspiration is gone," Lau says.

Interestingly, although the cookies are also popular abroad, and are currently shipped to France, Italy, Spain, Latin America, Israel, and the Middle East carrying messages in the appropriate tongue, an attempt to promote the cookie in China proved to be the Law's single export failure.

Since then, he's recycled his vast pile of philosophizing, although he's worried that readers will start to notice cookie comments that they've heard before, which could impair Wonton's edge on the competition. As a result, the company will soon be bringing in a new fortune cookie writer, and Lau will edit the results. His advice to future cookie fortune writers: "Don't have too complicated a mind, and think in 10-word sentences."

would involve a cold sweet mung bean or red bean porridge followed by chilled orange slices.

Fortune cookies are produced by machines that mix the dough, print messages, bake and cut the dough into discs, deposit a fortune at the center, and finally then mold the cookie into the dimpled form. In the old days, the cookies were handmade, but workers were injured by continual burns from the hot dough.

Most fortune cookie companies have only one person whose job it is to come up with the creative fortunes to be inserted into the cookies. The restrictions aren't too difficult, except that the fortune can only be about 11 words long (in order to fit onto the fortune), and the message must be positive, "you"-oriented, and fairly realistic. The old "You will travel across the water," has been replaced by more thoughtful or even inscrutable challenges, such as: "Those who walk in others' tracks leave no footprints." Others are simple observations: "You understand how to have fun with others and enjoy your solitude." Still others can be cautionary: "Rest is a good thing, but boredom is its brother."

Fortunes are sometimes composed by freelance writers, but today most companies employ their own writers who create sayings in response to social change and financial or political developments. In addition to a fortune, many fortune cookies also contain a Chinese phrase and a lucky number that is used by some enterprising superstitious diners as lottery numbers. It's this lucky number that turned out to be really lucky for 110 Chinese restaurant patrons, who won second place in the March 30, 2005 Powerball game. All the winners had picked five numbers correctly with no Powerball number, winning a total of

$19.4 million in unexpected payouts; 89 tickets won $100,000, but 21 additional tickets won $500,000 due to the Power Play multiplier option.

So unusual was the group of winners that Powerball officials thought they smelled a rat, until they traced the sequence to a fortune printed with the digits "22-28-32-33-39-40" and the prediction: "All the preparation you've done will finally be paying off." All the lucky winners had used those cookie numbers from fortune cookies made by Wonton Food Inc., a fortune cookie factory in Long Island City, Queens, New York, which reuses number combinations in thousands of cookies a day.

Pitfalls

There are very few openings for fortune writers—most seem to get the job because they already have a top job in the company, or because a relative asks them to do the job.

Perks

If you enjoy writing and are a closet philosopher, fortune cookie writing can be an enjoyable way to spend your days. Most such writers have a lot of independence and no one really looks over their shoulder to edit their work.

Get a Jump on the Job

There's no formal training involved in becoming a fortune cookie writer—you can't major in writing the pithy little philosophical snippets in college, for example. Your best bet would be to spend a lot of time writing and reading widely in philosophy (especially Chinese philosophy). Collect sayings and quotations you like and practice writing your own.

FUNERAL DIRECTOR

OVERVIEW

When someone dies and the family goes to a funeral home to arrange a funeral, the person they speak to is the funeral director (or mortician)—but speaking to the family and finalizing arrangements is only one small part of the funeral director's job. Funeral directors also move the body to a mortuary, prepare and embalm the remains, arrange for a ceremony to honor the person who died, and carry out final disposition of the remains.

Of course, a big part of a funeral director's job is to arrange the details of funerals. First, they'll interview the family about the ceremony, find out who should officiate, and establish the location, dates, and times of viewings, memorial services, and burials. Funeral directors also prepare obituaries for newspapers, arrange for pallbearers, schedule the opening and closing of a grave. They must also oversee the decoration of all funeral sites and provide transportation for the remains, mourners, and flowers between sites. If the deceased is to be buried in another state, it's the funeral director who handles those preparations as well.

Most states also allow funeral directors to practice embalming. Embalming is a cosmetic and preservative process that prepares the body for burial. If more than 24 hours pass between death and burial, state laws usually require that the body either be refrigerated or embalmed. Embalming has been practiced for thousands of years; while the specific

AT A GLANCE

Salary range

Salaries for funeral directors range from less than $26,470 a year to more than $85,910, plus paid holidays and vacation, health insurance, and a retirement plan. Specific wages vary by location, employer, and the funeral director's responsibilities.

Education/Experience

Funeral directors attend a mortuary science program for either a two-year associate degree or a four-year bachelor's degree; the American Board of Funeral Service Education accredits about 50 mortuary science programs. Most directors have a bachelor's degree in mortuary science, which usually includes courses in anatomy and physiology, pathology, embalming techniques, restorative art, business management, accounting, computers, and client services. There are also courses in the social sciences and legal, ethical, and regulatory subjects, such as psychology, grief counseling, oral and written communication, funeral service law, business law, and ethics. Most programs also provide information about funeral traditions and requirements in different cultures and religions. Funeral directors must complete a year-long internship or apprenticeship with a licensed funeral director or embalmer, learning how to handle and wash a body, inject embalming fluids, reconstruct or reshape body parts, and dress a body.

Personal Attributes

Funeral directors should be calm and professional, tactful, with the ability to communicate easily with the public. They should be exact and accurate in their work.

Requirements

A degree and an internship or apprenticeship, plus passage of a state licensing exam, are required. More than 30 states have requirements that funeral directors receive continuing education credits to maintain their licenses. Funeral directors who

(continues)

techniques and ceremonies may have been different, the practice of embalming has had a similar purpose since ancient times: to preserve and prepare the body for a respectful burial. Injecting embalming fluid is very similar to giving a blood transfusion, except it replaces the blood and fluid in the body with a preservative, helps clear out old blood, and restores a natural color and appearance to the body. It also slows down the decomposition process. The final process of embalming involves adding cosmetics to restore the natural appearance of the face.

Although it may seem to you that a career in mortuary science is depressing or gloomy because it focuses on death, people in this field do their best to honor and celebrate life. Carefully restoring and preserving the body, showing compassion for the grieving, and bringing loved ones together are all ways that they respect the grieving process while honoring the person who has died.

During the embalming process, the body is first washed and dried. After draining the blood from the body and replacing it with embalming fluid, the embalmer packs the body with chemical-soaked material to restore a more natural appearance, reshaping or reconstructing disfigured bodies using clay, cotton, plaster of Paris, or wax. Makeup may be applied if there is no cosmetologist.

Traditionally, funeral homes have been run as family businesses so that in the past, funeral directors often needed a family connection to get a job. Today, the best way for funeral directors to get hired is through connections made in mortuary school, which often are closely tied with local funeral homes. Schools can also help you get an internship while you're still in school, which often leads to permanent jobs.

The American Board of Funeral Service Education accredits about 50 mortuary science programs, most of which are two- or four-year programs. A few community and junior colleges offer two-year programs. Mortuary science programs include courses in anatomy, physiology,

---

Michele DeRosa, funeral director

Many funeral directors get into the business because it's simply what their family does and they've inherited a role, but Michele DeRosa is an example of the unusual case of someone who learned about the job from a nonrelative.

"I'm probably the odd case, but I got interested in [being a funeral director] when I was in high school," DeRosa says. "I knew a wonderful man in my hometown who operated a funeral home, and he really was the one who was my inspiration. He was a terrific teacher and taught me a lot before I decided to go to school for it. So many come into the job because of a family business, but those of us who choose the field might have a very different story as to why."

DeRosa is one of six funeral directors at Groff's Funeral Home in Lancaster, Pennsylvania, which has been in business since 1895. Once an independently-owned home with eight locations, it was eventually bought by a larger company. "In a family-owned business," she explains, "there is not always a generational flow. A funeral home owner may get old without a family member to take over, and may look for someone to purchase the business but allow them to stay active."

DeRosa has been a funeral director for the past 24 years, graduating from a mortuary science program at the University of Cincinnati. "Back then, it was a combined program, granting both a college degree and mortuary science degree." Eighteen years after getting her degree, DeRosa went back and got a bachelor's degree in psychology.

As a woman funeral director, DeRosa admits she has followed a nontraditional path. "The numbers [of women funeral directors] are growing, but certainly I was a pioneer," she says. At school and when she first graduated, she found it difficult to be accepted. "I understand why now," she says, "although initially I couldn't quite understand. Some funeral homes are in smaller, [more rural] locations, and there is sometimes a gender preference."

Luckily for her, she says, "I happened to come on board with a very open-minded funeral home, who welcomed me and accepted me and put me right on the schedule with male directors."

Unlike some people in the public who imagine the job must be depressing, DeRosa believes that she's actually working in a very service-oriented field. "You're able to help families start this journey that will affect the rest of their lives," she explains. "I think we have an opportunity to impact

---

pathology, embalming techniques, restorative art, business management, accounting, computers, client services, social sciences, psychology, grief counseling, oral and written communication, funeral service law, business law, and ethics.

Pitfalls

Although funeral directors wear protective gear such as lab coats, gloves, and face masks, they may be exposed to hazardous conditions, such as strong chemicals or contagious diseases or infections. The hours can be long and irregular, and you may need to work during evenings and weekends. Funeral service is a 24-hour, 7-day-a-week profession, although the workload is spread among all funeral home staff. Finally, funeral directors are only human, and many report that handling the funeral of a very young child can be emotionally difficult. Most funeral homes are small, family-run businesses, and like all self-employed people, funeral directors

their decisions or offer advice so that many months later, they look back on this experience as healing, and remember various parts of it. I think teens and young adults can be impacted strongly. It forms a foundation for how they look at this experience as they have other family or friends who die."

DeRosa does admit that there are cases in which employees become emotionally involved, and during those times it helps to have good support groups offered by the company.

For many directors, the job's downside is its hours. "Sometimes it's hard—it's a 24-hour, seven-day-a-week job," she explains. "Being on call can be difficult, but you know that it's part of your career. You kind of move forward from that. Sometimes you have to be committed to your job first; it supersedes your family, weekends, holiday events—but you know that going into it. There are a lot of jobs that are 24 hours a day, seven days a week, such as the police or an ambulance crew."

If you're interested in becoming a funeral director, DeRosa suggests that you check out your local funeral homes, talk with staff, and see if you can get a part-time position where you can observe. "That was my greatest help in getting into this field," she says. "I had a chance to get experience before choosing the route of going to school."

Some mortuary colleges would tell you there's a high percentage of people who go through the program and then decide it's not what they wanted, she explains. "I think those people envision the job in some ways that it may not be." That's why it's a good idea to observe, work with someone, and get some experience in the industry before going for a degree. Whether you can get an internship before you graduate depends on the state; some states allow you to do an internship first, but others require that you graduate first. In any case, there are always part-time positions in which you can soak up the environment, although you might not be able to meet with a family or do preparation work. You could work a viewing, handle the reception desk or help out with maintaining vehicles. This would allow you to have a mentor, so you can watch and listen.

"The reason we get into [the business] is because of the families we are serving, offering help and advice," she explains. "Sometimes people think because we're around death, it may affect our personalities or character. What it has done is made us aware how short life is and how valuable what we do is for people."

are responsible for the success or failure of their own business.

Perks

Most funeral directors believe they are performing a vital psychological service in helping family members through a very difficult yet important part of life. Rather than being gloomy, directors understand the importance of their role and that they have the opportunity to help a family in a very intimate way.

Get a Jump on the Job

If you're interested in becoming a funeral director, you should take courses in biology, chemistry, and public speaking—and plan to attend college. Working at a part-time or summer job at a funeral home as a funeral attendant or maintenance person, washing or polishing hearses, is a good way to find out what working in the funeral business is like.

FUNERAL HOME COSMETOLOGIST

OVERVIEW

"She looks so natural!" There's no higher compliment for a funeral home cosmetologist than to hear that a deceased loved one looks attractive during a viewing. A cosmetologist in the funeral home business is known as a *desairologist*—someone who is a licensed hairdresser/cosmetologist and who has studied the art and science of dressing the hair of and applying make-up on people who have died.

Although funeral homes in urban settings sometimes use local hairdresser services to come and do the hair and cosmetics for the deceased, most do their own cosmetic work as part of the normal preparation of the body. If the funeral home doesn't employ a cosmetologist, the embalmer works on the deceased's face to make it look natural.

During preparation, the desairologist checks with the director as to whether restoration and reconstructive treatments were performed to the dead person's eyes, mouth, and different areas of the face, including the hairline.

A mortuary cream is applied to the person's face, neck, and hands; the cream is removed when the foundation base is applied, and helps the foundation adhere to the skin, adding softness and color. The dead person's facial skin is almost always in good condition, in part as the result of the embalming procedures.

Old cosmetics are removed, and any stray hairs found in the area of the face or under the chin are cut. The desairologist uses a cosmetic kit containing an assort-

ment of foundations, finishing powders, eyebrow pencils, and numerous cosmetic brushes that are designed to be effective for a wide range of skin color and pH or body temperatures.

A desairologist then applies makeup to cover unnatural skin tones and blemishes, along with lip color and sometimes hair color. To achieve color balance, the person's facial features are viewed from different angles, and facial features are highlighted with a color base two or three shades darker than the foundation. A receding chin and deep sunken or dark circles under the eyes can be improved with corrective makeup, to help achieve a natural look to the face.

A finishing powder is then dusted on the face and neck, and an eyebrow pencil is stroked back and forth over the lashes and eyebrows to blend and remove remaining

Barbara Benn Spada, licensed desairologist

For Barbara Benn Spada, her work as a desairologist all started when she helped out a friend who had a job at a local funeral home. Spada had studied hairdressing and cosmetology in Boston, Hartford, and New York City, and had served an extensive apprenticeship in Milan, Italy, where she also studied esthetics. Over the years, with her own salons and later as a manager of a large full-service salon, she attended classes at a local state college to become certified in vocational/technical (vo/tech) education, doing her student teaching at a local state vo/tech high school. Later, she taught full time at a private hairdressing and cosmetology school, eventually becoming director of another hairdresser/barber/cosmetology accredited two-year career college.

"The hairdressing/cosmetologist field is wonderful for those interested in health, science, beauty, and fashion," she says. "I worked many hair shows/conventions teaching other professionals about professional products in private seminars and classes." All of this experience and background became significant when she started helping a friend who had a funeral call at a funeral home. "As that business grew, I became more involved," she says. "One must be willing to be flexible, since 'death calls' have no timetable. Until [the embalming] is completed, and the dressing and casketing has taken place; our services must wait. Sometimes, you get a late night or early morning call to return to do a 'touch up'!"

Currently, Spada is a licensed cosmetologist working at the Paul A. Shaker funeral home in New Britain, Connecticut, although she sometimes works for other funeral homes, and she still works one day a week with live clients.

It's vital to be absolutely confidential and private about the work being done, she explains, and it's also important to be accurate, low key, prepared, and on time. "A funeral requires as many details to plan and arrange as a wedding . . . only, we only have a few days instead of a year or so, and no rehearsals. So everyone is a part of the final product. Teamwork is essential. Professionalism is the keynote here."

The constant, tremendous pressure can be difficult, particularly when there are several calls at once. But the most difficult part of the business for everyone—funeral directors, embalmers, and staff—is handling the funeral of an infant or child. "In 13 years, I don't recall if I have ever gone to the church and cemetery with the families," she says. "What I do here at the funeral home is difficult enough. Especially when we are dealing with the families from the initial call."

What she likes best are the interactions with the friends and family of the deceased. "It's a rewarding feeling when the families thank you in person and letters for the comfort you gave them when viewing their loved ones for the last time," she says. "It means a lot when visitors to a wake walk up to you and thank you personally for restoring the loved one, so a lasting good memory will perhaps erase one of illness. You truly feel you have eased the pain of the families through some of their darkest hours."

If you're truly interested in working for a funeral home as a licensed hairdresser, Spada says you'll need to accept the fact that it will be a part-time, as-needed kind of job. "However, if you want a career in the mortuary sciences fields and want to specialize more in restorative arts, I'd advise students to enroll in a mortuary arts program and take a hairdressing/cosmetology class as a backup."

(continues)

(continued)

Once you're proficient in all phases of hairdressing (including coloring, cutting, styling, weaving, wigs, and hairpieces), and you've passed a state board exam and fulfilled all the educational standards, you should send out a resume of your skills to a funeral home, attach a copy of your personal business card, and ask to be interviewed and given the opportunity to demonstrate your skills. Often, you'll be asked to give your professional opinions to the funeral home staff on what further preparation could be done to enhance the person's final look.

"Once the funeral director has met with a family making the final arrangements, and you may or may not have a great photo to work from, you are often left to your own imagination and resources to find ways to enhance the final appearance of the deceased," she says. This is not the time to show up with messy hair and torn blue jeans. "Even if you never meet the family, funeral home employees must be professionally attired. This includes 'casual help' such as part-timers, hairdressers, livery, and doormen.

"The funeral director will be the person who will ultimately assist the family as they have the initial viewing," she says. "If any changes must be made, the hairdresser must return."

Like most individuals in the funeral industry, she doesn't think of the business as depressing. "I view it as responsible, comforting, and necessary," she explains. "Both the living and the deceased need a hairdresser.

"Everyone sooner or later has to deal with the death of friends and family," she says. "So if in the final moments a family can focus on the good memories and we can assist them through the final process of one's last goodbye and have them come away from the funeral feeling that their last 'visit' with their loved one was a comfort, then we have truly done our job as a team. Wakes and funerals are truly for the living—the survivors.

"This field, whether you greet visitors at the door for wakes and funerals or you're a licensed embalmer/funeral director—even the office staff, hairdressers, and livery—is definitely not for the faint of heart, flighty, or non-motivated. It is a challenging, very intense field, but you must be willing to sacrifice a lot of free time—no regular schedules or holidays or weekends off! It's a business unlike any I have ever been in contact with. But I wouldn't trade it for the world!"

powder. A liquid dry-wash is used to absorb any foundation base that may have seeped at the hairline.

Finally, the desairologist also styles the person's hair to help give a natural appearance to someone who has died. Adding costume jewelry or eyeglasses that may have been sent to the funeral home is the final step in preparing the body.

Although hairdressing and makeup are only a very small part of the complete funeral, they are very important parts. In the end, it won't matter how nice the funeral home and grounds look—if the body doesn't look good, the family won't be happy.

Pitfalls

It's not every cosmetologist who can feel comfortable applying makeup on a dead person, and for emotional reasons this job is not for everyone. In addition, the unpredictable hours can be a problem; desairologists usually work on an on-call basis for smaller funeral homes; large corporate homes typically like to have a skilled embalmer on staff who can handle all the embalming and cosmetic applications, unless the family requests a special hair service or their own licensed hairdresser. Unless you can work long late hours under an extreme amount of stress and work well with the grieving public, it's probably a better idea to stay in the hair salon.

Perks

It can be emotionally satisfying to know that your work truly helps grieving friends and family feel better when they look at a deceased loved one and see a "natural" appearance. Most desairologists truly feel that they are performing a very important service for the grieving public, and helping people during a very emotionally draining time. Especially if the deceased has been ill for a long time, achieving a natural, peaceful, and healthy look can make those left behind form comforting memories when saying goodbye to someone who has died.

Get a Jump on the Job

If you're interested in desairology, you'll first need to be a licensed cosmetologist or hairdresser. See if you can work part-time at a salon, and read all you can about working as a desairologist. Some funeral homes may let you observe, and if this is the case you can get an idea of whether you'd like to do this work for a career.

GOVERNESS

OVERVIEW

To Americans, the job of governess may seem like something straight out of a Victorian novel, but even today many families across the country hire a governess to help educate the children and take care of them during working hours.

Sounds like a nanny, right? But a nanny needs only a high school diploma to take care of children (often including infants). A governess must have a bachelor's degree, and the position emphasizes education, not child care. A governess is really a private educator with no household responsibilities. However, they are responsible for the children, so modern governesses see that the child's laundry is done, and may prepare breakfast and lunch for the child if they are alone with them in the house. But if the child's parents employ a full staff, the governess won't cook.

Although a governess doesn't really need to live in, most families provide very nice living quarters and sometimes provide private apartments for their governesses. A governess typically will relocate and live with a family, traveling with them on holidays as well. Some governesses make this a career, while others simply work at this job for a few years, using it as a stepping stone to other work.

Even if the family includes very young infants, the governess is teaching all the time. If the children in the family are in school, the governess helps with homework or activities after school.

Graduates of a governess program typically complete a three-month academic program of classroom instruction and gain further experience with children and families through an in-home practicum and nine-month externship.

Pitfalls

If there isn't a good "fit" between governess and family, the job can be stressful and difficult. It also requires a lot of patience; it can be difficult if the governess' idea of how to raise a child differs significantly from the ideas of the parent, putting the two in direct conflict. If a strong bond develops between governess and child, the parent may become jealous.

Rachel Rock, governess

Rachel Rock was almost at the end of her college years at Hillsdale College when some of her roommates visited a job fair and met representatives from a nanny/governess school. "They came back all excited about this totally unusual job," she recalls, "and I was ecstatic." She'd been looking for something unusual and different, and to Rachel Rock, becoming a governess was just the sort of unusual job she'd been hoping for.

"One of my roommates went with me to the school (the English Nanny and Governess School) and I decided to attend their three-month program." The governess course was an intensive program of constantly changing subjects, including child development, first aid, music, singing, storytelling, and driving. The school also offers a lifelong placement program so a grad can call at any time and find a family who needs a governess. Midway through the program, Rock started doing interviews and looking up potential families. Once the student submits a list of people in whom she's interested, Rock explains, the school tries to match her with a good family. "That's the biggest part of the job, finding someone you can click with," Rock says. "[The school] needs to get to know you a little bit before they can do that."

From time to time, Rock still checks out the online job openings just for fun, and recently noted that a king and queen of a small European country were looking for an American governess—apparently now seen as more desirable than a traditional English governess.

Rock, a native of Michigan, was matched with a family in Manhattan. "I've had the best time of my life," she says, "experiencing everything. I have a couple of college buddies here, and they are struggling, because it's expensive to live in the city. I get to float along here."

Rock has been with her first family as governess for a little over a year and half. "I plan to stick with them probably until I'm done with the career," she says, not envisioning herself moving on to be governess with a second family. She takes care of two small boys, ages 4 and 6, and says that your experience of being a governess truly depends on the family for whom you work.

"With this one, the mom and I have clicked so well, she's mentioned my staying on after the kids are gone, and opening a business together," Rock says. "The kinds of jobs a governess does really depends on what the kids' needs are," she says. "It all depends on what the situation is. I would say the majority of times, families want someone to help with kids after school for tutoring, or for the infant stages."

Rock does not live with her family, but instead lives with the children's grandmother a few doors down. "So I'm still rent free, with my own space," she says. She's expected to work 50 weeks a year, Monday through Friday, 10 hours day—but during the middle of the day she gets a three-hour break. She's at the house when the kids are in school, tidying up and washing the children's clothes.

"I love the fact that I can wake up every day and look forward to going to work," she says. "I truly just enjoy myself every single day and that's the best part about it. I can do what I'd like to do, and these kids are amazing. I'm helping them grow. They actually understand, and they thank you. One of the boys told me: 'You're going to go to heaven because we know our presidents.' They're amazing kids."

(continues)

(continued)

Of course, sometimes the job isn't easy. Rock says some governesses she knows endure personality clashes. "It's difficult for them to have to work with someone [they] disagree with," she explains. "If you disagree with the way [the parents are] raising their kids, you can't stop them. You have to do what you think is right, without totally offending the parent, who's in control."

Rock's advice for anyone interested in being a governess is to go into the job with your eyes open. "I'd say the biggest thing is, don't get caught up in what [the job] looks like, or what you imagine it would be like. If you picture yourself in an extravagant lifestyle, where you think about lying in the sun having drinks brought to you, you'll be miserable, because you're the one bringing the drinks."

Rock, who was an international studies major in college, reasoned that working as a governess would allow her to save up enough money to start her own business. "I also love being with kids; I would have loved being a teacher, but I'm awful in a classroom." Her dreams of owning her own business are on the back burner for now, she says, but she hopes to do it one day.

Perks

If you love kids and you love teaching, being a governess can be financially rewarding and open up a totally different world than anything you've experienced before. Many families take their governesses on vacation or travel with them, and so you'll get to see many parts of the world you might otherwise have missed.

Get a Jump on the Job

You'll need a solid university education with an emphasis on early childhood learning if you want to be a governess, so you'll need to work hard in school. Take lots of babysitting jobs and work with kids in camps or other summer programs whenever possible. The more you know and understand about younger children, the better you'll know whether this career is for you.

HOLIDAY DECORATOR

OVERVIEW

Outdoing the neighbors when it comes to holiday lights and decorations is the plot of at least a few movies and sitcoms. But the things people are willing to do when it comes to outdoing the neighbors is no laughing matter; it's big business. Christmas decorating has become close to a billion-dollar-a-year industry. It's not only homeowners getting into the spirit; retailers also know that decorations boost sales by putting shoppers in a holiday mood. Everyone from hotels to corporate offices, banks to doctors' offices, is hanging up the holiday lights and spreading some holiday cheer.

But not everyone has the time or inclination to climb on a ladder and hang hundreds of twinkle lights from their eaves. That is where the holiday decorator comes in. For a fee, the decorator and his team will turn your surroundings into Santa's workshop, a winter wonderland, or whatever your heart desires.

As more and more parents are both working outside of the home, trying to juggle schedules filled with ballet practice, soccer games, and piano lessons, more and more people are turning to holiday decorators to create the holiday of their dreams. And that's exactly what most holiday decorators will do. While many customers are only looking for someone to decorate the outsides of their homes, preferring to do the interior decorating themselves, there are customers who want everything done—inside and out.

The first contact between the decorator and the customer will be an estimate/

AT A GLANCE

Salary Range

A holiday decorator can make as much as $60,000 to $70,000 or more a year. The amount depends greatly on a number of things including the geographic location, the customer base, and the services that the decorator offers. Like many other independent businesses, the salary also depends in part on how much time and energy the owner puts into making it a success.

Education/Experience

None required. A good working knowledge and understanding of electricity is helpful. Many holiday decorators own their own businesses, so classes in management, accounting, marketing, and other business-related topics would be very helpful.

Personal Attributes

Holiday decorators need to be creative and detail-oriented. They need to be willing to work hard to get the job done quickly and correctly the first time. Holiday decorators need to be customer-oriented with good people skills. They need to be physically able to climb up and down ladders with equipment and to work at heights installing lights and other display items, and they need to be conscious of safety concerns while doing their job. They also need to be willing and able to work outside in all types of weather.

Requirements

Self-employed holiday decorators will most likely need to file Doing Business As (DBA) papers, get a tax license, and acquire any other local permits required under local and/or state ordinances. They also need to be aware of any local ordinances limiting the size of holiday displays. Holiday decorators need to carry liability insurance to cover themselves and any employees they have in case they are injured on the job.

Outlook

Hiring someone to come in and do holiday decorating is a relatively new trend, but one that

(continues)

consultation at the customer's home or business (depending on which the decorator will be decorating). The customer will give the decorator an idea how much he is willing to spend on decorating and will let the decorator know any specific ideas, designs, or elements he would like included in the display. If the customer isn't sure what he wants, he might look through a portfolio with pictures of other jobs the decorator has done, picking and choosing designs and elements that he likes. Then the decorator will take that budget and the customer's ideas and design a plan that can be done within the budgeted amount. Some individuals are only able to spend a few hundred dollars on decorating, while others spend $25,000 or more to have the house or business decked out for the season. Many decorators offer the estimate/consultation as a free service to their customers, realizing that more people are apt to call someone to give them a free estimate before calling someone who charges for the same service.

Once the customer has settled on a decorating plan that fits his budget and wants, the decorator will draw up an installation plan. Lights can be time consuming to put up, but they aren't really noticeable until they are lit, so the decorator and his team may install lights on the building and in the trees during the fall. This is especially true if the decorator is looking at a large job, or the decorator is working in an area with inclement weather during November and December. However, since most customers don't really want a large blow-up snowman on their lawns while the leaves are still falling from the trees, the decorator and his team usually return right before or after Thanksgiving (depending on when the customer wants the decorating complete) to install the visible holiday items and the greenery.

Even when the decorating is done, the decorator and his team still have work to do. They will check on the customers' displays several times during the season to repair or replace items that stop working. Most decorators are on call seven days a week during the time that their customers' displays are lit in case something goes wrong in between checkups. Many decorators will work to get displays working as quickly as possible to make the customer happy.

After the holiday, the decorator and his team will return to remove the seasonal items and greenery as quickly as possible. After all, who really wants Santa Claus greeting their Super Bowl party guests in late January? The lights are usually removed in the spring.

Many holiday decorators offer their customers a free storage service built into the total cost of their service. After the items are removed from the customer's home or business, items that can be used again (usually everything except live greenery) are checked for damage and then packed away ready for next season. Many holiday decorators prefer not to rent items or to use things that the customer already owns, because the decorator has no way of ensuring that the items will work prop-

Brad Finkle, holiday decorator

Like many families, the Finkles enjoyed their annual Christmas Eve drive to enjoy the holiday lights and decorations. It's that family tradition that Brad Finkle credits with landing him in his present-day profession. "I was crazy about the lights and decorations, and I got the bug."

Like many holiday decorators and would-be decorators, Finkle started out decorating his parents' home; that was more than 25 years ago now. Finkle admits, "I'm the type of person to do it overboard and take it to the next level." His displays got noticed, and soon neighbors were asking for help. "The next thing I knew people were paying me and the light bulb went off. I could make this a business."

Finkle comes by his entrepreneurial nature quite naturally; his dad also owned his own business. Finkle worked all sorts of jobs throughout high school, and when it came time for college, he didn't go. "I got a taste of money in high school, and I liked it," he says about his decision. Finkle ran a haunted house for a while, and did other seasonal work, but he always enjoyed decorating for Christmas more than any other job he had.

Even though he's now getting paid to do what he loves, if Finkle had his way there is at least one thing he'd change—a longer set-up season. Finkle has to squeeze three months worth of work into about one month each fall. That often means working from 6 a.m. to 6 p.m. or later, seven days a week, from mid-October to the first of December.

With such a tight time frame, Finkle says there is a lot of pressure. "You have to be organized and hit the ground running," he says. "You have to have everything ready so that everything flows, because you have deadlines to meet. And you never know if Mother Nature will cooperate." Finkle speaks from experience on the last point; his company is in Omaha, Nebraska.

But, even for all the hard work, stress, and inclement weather Finkle endures, there is nothing like getting the job done. "After everything is set up, I sit in my car and watch the faces of the people, both kids and adults, who come to look at the lights and decorations; families carrying on the tradition just like I did as a child." For Finkle, that makes it all worthwhile.

As for the future of holiday decorating, Finkle believes that now is a great time to get into it. Because of media attention, people are learning that you can actually hire someone to decorate your house for the holidays. At his own company, Finkle says people are starting to call earlier and earlier each year. "A company can only decorate so many houses," he says. "There is more than enough work for more than one company in an area," adding that even he has more calls than he can take on.

So, what advice does Finkle offer to someone hoping to jump into this growing profession? "Start out small and don't jump in without knowing what you're doing. Start with a few accounts and grow from there. If you take on too much, your customers will suffer. Take it slow and make sure you do the job right the first time." Finkle says there are some things to learn, but they can easily be mastered within a few years. "It's something you can have a lot of fun with, especially if you are creative."

To see some of Finkle's spectacular lighting displays, check out the gallery at his Web site, http://www.creativedecoratinginc.com.

erly during the time the house or business is decorated. Instead, the decorator sells the customer quality items to use in the display.

For some, holiday decorating is a seasonal job. Many lawn care companies, nurseries, construction companies, pool service companies, and others provide decorating services during a time when business is traditionally slow. For others, holiday decorating is a full-time business, with those decorators attending trade shows, designing displays for family and friends, and expanding their customer base.

To keep up-to-date on the latest advances in holiday decorating, decorators can attend the Holiday & Home Expo each January in Dallas. Decorators also have the option of Plantscape's biennial conference held in June of even years in Pittsburgh. The conference offers training sessions covering a wide range of interior and exterior decorating topics. Decorators can win cash prizes by entering projects in the National Business Christmas Decorators Awards Contest.

No formal education or training is required to become a holiday decorator. If you decided to go into the holiday decorating business, you might choose to buy into a franchise or open your own independent business. A franchise can be very expensive, but you get an established company name, company training and support, referrals, and advertising benefits. Many franchises also offer the guarantee of a protected area, meaning they won't sell someone else a franchise in your area. That doesn't mean that you couldn't have competition from independent decorators.

If you start your own company, your start-up costs will be very low (you don't even need a storefront—just some ladders and other tools). You'll probably also want to invest in a small inventory of lights, but if money is tight you can always buy what you need once you have a signed contract with a customer. You'll have to work hard to build a solid client base if you start out on your own.

As your business grows, you may decide to expand to holidays other than Christmas, which is getting more and more popular each year. Soon there may definitely be a market for holiday decorators year-round. You might also decide to open a storefront where you can show off what's new in holiday decorating along with showcasing your own holiday designs.

Pitfalls

Holiday decorators may be on call seven days a week during the holiday season in case their customers have problems. With such a short time frame in which to get the work done, holiday decorators often have to work outside in inclement weather to meet their deadlines.

Perks

Holiday decorators have the honor of turning someone's dream holiday into reality. People everywhere decorate for the holidays, so anyone could start a holiday decorating business. Start-up costs are low, and holiday decorating can be a seasonal job, allowing decorators to pursue other interests or business possibilities during the off-season.

Get a Jump on the Job

Volunteer to decorate your family's house for the holiday as well as the homes of relatives and neighbors. Take pictures and start building a portfolio. As your skills improve, offer your skills to area schools, service agencies, businesses, and more. Add pictures and letters of recommendation to your portfolio. Look for seasonal work with a holiday decorator if possible. Consider taking business, advertising, and marketing classes in high school or at a local junior or community college.

HOME STAGER

OVERVIEW

When it's time to sell the house, most people tidy up and call the real estate agent, but there's one more thing homeowners should do when they decide to put their house on the market, and that's call a home stager. If you've never heard of a home stager, you're not alone.

The concept was invented in the 1970s by Barb Schwarz, an interior decorator turned real estate agent who developed a system that would allow agents to help sellers prepare their homes to sell without offending them. Her idea was to "stage the home for sale," or to "set the stage." The notion was so unique that Schwarz eventually went on to trademark the term *stage* in terms of real estate and preparing a home for sale. Even though it's been around for more than 30 years, actually hiring someone to come in and help you get your house ready to sell is still a foreign idea to many people.

When you stage a home, you prepare it so it will sell quickly for the best price. Staging is different for each house, but it usually involves small, inexpensive changes that will make a big impact: things such as re-arranging furniture, painting a wall or trim, removing pictures, or adding plants or flowers. Surveys show that a staged home may sell up to 20 times faster than an un-staged home, for at least a 3 percent higher price. Homeowners who invested a small amount in staging their homes saw an average return of close to 170 percent.

At a first meeting with a new client, the stager might share with the homeowner her portfolio, showing "before" and "after" pictures of houses on which he or she has worked. If possible, the stager also may share information showing how quickly the home sold after it was staged, as well as letters of recommendation from happy clients. At this first meeting, the stager will also detail the services as well as the fee schedule.

One of the services that stagers offer is a consultation. During a consultation visit, the stager will tour the home with the homeowner, taking extensive notes. The stager also walks around the outside of the house, making notes on ways to improve the curb appeal of the property. Then the stager prepares a recommendations report—an in-depth list of specific changes for the homeowner to make. The recommendations report might suggest removing specific pieces of furniture and rearranging the remaining pieces in a specific way to make the room look more inviting, hanging a mirror to make a room feel bigger, painting the front door a different color to make the home more welcoming, or removing pictures of the homeowner's family so that potential buyers can picture themselves in the home. The stager will then prepare and deliver the report very quickly after the consultation, usually within a few days. After the homeowner has had a chance to make the changes, most stagers will return to add a few personal touches and take photographs to be used to market the house. The consultation service is great for the homeowner with the time and know-how to invest in getting the house ready to sell.

However, not everyone has the time, knowledge, or the desire to do the work required to get a home ready to put on the market. For that reason, most stagers will come in and make the changes for the homeowner, rearranging the furniture, de-cluttering, and so on. Some stagers will even shop for the accessories they feel are needed to "set the stage." However, stagers generally will not clean the house or pack the items they feel need to be removed.

Stagers' services vary from person to person, depending in part upon what the stager's strengths are, and what the market will support (or what people are willing to pay for). Some stagers stage commercial offices, presenting a great first impression to clients. Some stagers even offer seasonal staging services.

For some, home staging is a part-time job. With the flexible scheduling it allows, it's a good option for someone interested in only working part time. Some interior decorators offer staging services as an extension of their day-to-day remodeling businesses. Some real estate agents also learn the ins and outs of staging as an additional benefit that they can offer their clients, for an additional fee. For others, home staging is a full-time business, with those stagers devoting time and energy to building their businesses and expanding their customer base.

No formal education or training is required to become a home stager, but it will be very difficult to get into the business, much less build a client base, without some training. You can become an accredited staging professional (ASP) by completing an intensive three-day training program. Training includes two-and-a-half days of classroom instruction and a half-day actually staging a house. In addition to learning how to stage, classroom instruction includes sessions on how to set up your business, pricing, marketing, bidding, and other business-related topics. Courses are taught throughout the year at locations around the United States by certified accredited staging professional trainers (CASPTs).

Shelley Wagner, home stager and ASP course trainer, ASPM

Home staging is a way to prepare a home for sale within the seller's budget so it sells quicker and for top dollar," explains stager Shelley Wagner, with an enthusiasm for her career that is unmistakable. Staging is not decorating; it's actually the opposite of decorating. "Whereas decorating is personal, staging is impersonal," she explains. Staging prepares the house so that it appeals to the broadest range of buyers. "It mentally allows the buyer to see themselves in the house," she says. "It allows them to mentally move in."

Wagner seems to come by her talent for staging naturally. As a young newlywed with no money to spend on furniture and accessories, she learned how to use what she had to create the look she wanted. Impressed with her results, friends and family began asking her to do the same for them. Eventually she opened her own room redesign business. More than a decade later, Wagner learned about home staging on the Internet in 2003, and she has skyrocketed to the top of her profession. Wagner started with the ASP class in Chicago, the closest location to her metro-Detroit home. Six months later, she was in Concord, California for the Master's class with Barb Schwarz. Six months after that, she was asked to become an ASP trainer. Now, in addition to staging houses, Wagner travels around the country training others how to become a home stager.

That Internet discovery was truly life-changing for Wagner. "Staging has changed my life, how I live, and how I communicate," she says. "I love, love, love staging! We're the last profession to make house calls."

But it's no laughing matter when asked what she enjoys most about the job. With passion, Wagner says it's really all about helping people. She explains that through her services, she really changes peoples' lives, because when homeowners sell a house for top dollar, they may be able to send a child to college, retire early, buy something special, or do something else that they never thought possible. "It's a win-win situation for everyone, and it's a great joy to see other people's happiness. It's powerful."

But helping people doesn't stop when the work day is over; Wagner and other ASPs give back to their communities in their free time. In September 2005, Wagner and other members of the Great Lakes chapter of the IAHSP (the regional chapter Wagner founded) volunteered their time during the first annual Community Worldwide Staging Service Day. Members staged rooms for the girls at The Children's Home of Detroit.

"Staging is a great [career] option for a lot of people," she says. If you're interested in becoming a home stager, Wagner suggests shadowing a stager, talking to people in the business, doing your research. "Go for it," she says. "It'll be the best business decision you ever made.

"Look for your life's work. Identify the gift in you and find a way to serve others with that life. Therein lays your purpose, your success, and your happiness."

To see some of Wagner's before and after pictures, and see if she's teaching a class near you, visit her Web site at http://www.setthestagenow.com.

After becoming an APS, stagers can train to become an accredited staging professional master (ASPM). The ASPM program (also called the Master's course) involves six days studying with Barb Schwarz, the developer of the staged home concept. If you are fortunate to be able to take the ASP class with Schwarz, then it is only an additional three days of study to earn your ASPM designation, which requires a total of six days studying with Schwarz.

Real estate agents looking to give their homes an advantage on the market may consider enrolling in the ASP Realtor program. In the two-day program, real estate agents will learn how to help their clients get their homes ready to put on the market so that the home sells faster; and for as much money as possible.

After becoming an ASP, individuals can join the International Association of Home Staging Professionals (IAHSP). Membership allows ASPs to network with other ASPs through regional chapters, conference calls, and conventions. These opportunities give members opportunities to share ideas, discuss staging-related issues, participate in training, as well as inspire and motivate one another. Members stay up-to-date on the most current advances in staging through the IAHSP newsletter which also includes information on upcoming events, new products, ideas that really work, and articles written by fellow members.

Pitfalls

Stagers may have difficulty making a full-time living in rural or small suburban areas. You may need to consider relocating if you hope to make a living as a stager. Occasionally, dealing with some customers can be very stressful.

Perks

A home stager's work makes it possible for the homeowners to sell their homes; helping turn the dream of moving into a reality. People everywhere sell their homes, so it may be possible for a stager to find at least part-time work in his or her present area without relocating. Staging can be a part-time job, allowing stagers who choose, to pursue other interests or business possibilities during their free time.

Get a Jump on the Job

Consider taking classes in business, advertising, accounting, marketing, and interior design in high school or at a local junior or community college. If possible, job-shadow a stager for several days or longer, or look for a summer job working for a stager.

HOTEL CONCIERGE

OVERVIEW

When you're in a strange city and you want something to do, you can just pick up a travel guide or watch your hotel's "information" channel on TV, or you can trot downstairs and chat with your hotel's concierge for advice about the local flora and fauna.

The nice thing about concierges is that they have actually been to most of the restaurants and sights in the city, so they can tell you whether you'll feel uncomfortable wearing a tux to a casual diner, or what kind of crowd frequents a local nightclub. It's kind of like having a best friend down at the front desk, ready to give you the inside information on the best places to go and things to do.

The concierge also coordinates all guest requests for special arrangements or services, courteously and efficiently, and informs guests of hotel services, features, and room amenities. They should be experts on the city in which they work, serving almost as a tour guide and travel expert. Basically, a concierge takes care of all those annoying details that a guest doesn't have time for or doesn't know how to do, acting as a sort of butler for the entire hotel. What most travelers don't realize is that you don't even have to be a guest at the hotel where a concierge works to benefit from these services. A professional concierge's job is to help anyone who asks for advice or help—willingly, politely, and knowledgeably. A concierge from Hotel A would not even blink an eye if a guest from Hotel B stopped by for assistance.

AT A GLANCE

Salary Range
Between $20,000 and $50,000 a year, plus significant tips, along with incentives such as commissions from taxis, free meals in the hotel restaurant. Tips can be substantial and make up a good part of your income.

Education/Experience
Most training is learned on the job; customer service background helpful.

Personal Attributes
You need to be tenacious, diplomatic, articulate, thoughtful, sincere, and calm in the face of stress, with an inquisitive nature, an outgoing personality, and interest in organizing events for others. You should also be friendly, knowledgeable, and detail-oriented. You'll need to be able to function well in a fast-paced environment under considerable pressure, with a broad-based personal knowledge of the area and all it has to offer.

Requirements
Hotel concierges need good written and oral communication skills and excellent telephone etiquette. Knowing several languages is helpful in large, big-city hotels.

Outlook
The number of concierge jobs is expected to increase, as customers become more familiar with the concierge idea.

This help can include almost any special or personal services for guests, including taking messages, arranging for babysitting, making hotel reservations in other cities, arranging for or giving advice on entertainment, and monitoring requests for housekeeping and maintenance.

They may tell guests about nearby events, sites, or historical monuments and other areas of interest, and discuss great

Glen Pappas, concierge

Glen Pappas was an 18-year veteran of the hotel industry when he fell into the job of concierge by accident—and he's been doing it ever since. Armed with a bachelor's degree in hospitality management, he worked as housekeeping supervisor and executive housekeeper for a number of big-city hotels. Once he landed in Washington, D.C., as a front desk clerk, his supervisor noted his superior human relations skills and suggested he might be good concierge material. Being a concierge is more than a matter of handing out maps and restaurant guides—it requires excellent guest service skills, patience, and a friendly, outgoing personality. "They saw my skills were good and I was patient," Pappas says. "My supervisor said, 'Could you do it?' and I said 'Sure!'" Pappas says. "That was June 1995, and I've been a concierge ever since!"

Pappas, who now works as concierge at the Hyatt Regency Penn's Landing in Philadelphia, says he was lucky to have a good mentor when he started out. "She gave me a good early base," he says. "I would chat and ask her a lot of questions. There's no real educational degree you can get to be a concierge. Your best education is how you were raised, did you travel and get to see things, do you like history. I took a bunch of American history courses. And working first as a desk clerk is a good idea." The job of a hotel concierge isn't just in getting tickets and providing information—it's also to help out any hotel client with any sort of problem. "The hardest part of your first year on the job is learning your way around." Whenever he moves to a new city to take a new concierge job, he tries to immerse himself in the history of the city. This allows him to chat knowledgably with his guests and point out interesting historical sights they might want to see.

Being a concierge is a job Pappas truly enjoys. "I love the contact with different people," he says, which is the reason he prefers working for a hotel instead of for a residential building. In a hotel, the clients are always changing. "There are always a few people you may have trouble dealing with," he says, "but you know you'll only have them for a few days."

A degree in hotel services isn't really necessary to becoming a concierge, as long as you're well-rounded, he says. "I'm a movie nut, and I see almost everything. So I can usually give my opinion about a movie. You've also got to be willing to go into a lot of different restaurants and try their food. I'll be honest—I don't really like Mexican food. So when I'm asked for a recommendation for a Mexican restaurant, I give someone else's recommendation. My customer is the most important thing to me," he says, "I'm more choosey about what I recommend. Ultimately, I want my guest to be happy.

"There's very little that shocks me anymore," he says, "I always get people saying: 'I'm looking for this or that.' Of course, I can't do anything illegal. I had an Italian family who wanted a particular kind of dog fence to take home to Italy. We tracked them down and they told us how to handle finding the fence on the east coast. The family wanted to pay cash, so I drove to Baltimore to purchase it for them.

"The job is all about using contacts and exchanging favors with others in the business," he says. "I've given people my own clothes, my own tux, because theirs got lost. I've made my other half pick up a client and take them to the closest tux place. I had a gentleman who wanted to rent a Mercedes, but Philadelphia doesn't have rental agencies like that. I went to New York City for him to get the car." Although every job has a few negative points about it, Pappas says, he enjoys most things about being a concierge. He likes dealing directly with clients, and in particular, he loves a challenge. "I keep going until I find out whatever it is I don't know," he says.

places to eat. Concierges also coordinate all guest requests for special arrangements or services, and describe hotel services, features, and room amenities. They can serve almost as a mini tour guide and travel expert. In short, a concierge takes care of all those annoying details that a guest doesn't have time for or doesn't know how to do.

Although more and more people are getting used to working with a concierge, very few know where this customer service–based profession originated. The word *concierge* evolves from the French *comte des cierges*, the "keeper of the candles," a term that referred to the servant who attended to the whims of visiting noblemen at medieval castles. Eventually, the name concierge came to stand for "keeper of the keys" at hotels. There is even a famous prison in Paris that is called The Conciergerie, in honor of the warden who kept the keys and assigned cells to the inmates. In France, the concierge was always the resident in an apartment building who served as a doorkeeper and landlord's representative. Eventually, the term was adopted by large hotels around the world who took the French concierge idea and began offering the sort of "doorkeeper" service to their guests.

Concierges will fill any request as long as it's legal, ethical, and appropriate. This might mean tracking down lost airline tickets, picking up an item from a local store, or arranging for a rare bottle of wine to be delivered to a client entertaining a business customer. Some of the most innovative services that a hotel concierge can perform involve handling those last-minute crises smoothly and efficiently—and you never know what that may be. For ex-

ample, 30 minutes before a hotel guest is expected to meet a business associate, she may come to you with ink on her blouse, and you'll be expected to come up with a new blouse. Many concierges spend a lot of their own time looking at the city from a guest's point of view, because they truly enjoy being a sort of ambassador for their town or city.

Pitfalls

In the hotel business, you will definitely need to work nights and weekends, and your schedule may vary from week to week. Most concierges also stand at their lobby desks all day, which can be tiring.

Perks

This type of job can be very rewarding, both personally and financially, since you can earn significant tips in addition to your hourly salary. A very experienced concierge can earn a six-figure income as he or she rises in seniority. If you enjoy people and you love tracking down information—and you've got lots of connections—this can be a great job. No two days in the life of a concierge are the same.

Get a Jump on the Job

A good way to get started in the business is by working at a hotel's front desk, watching and listening to an experienced concierge, who is usually located close to the front desk. Try going to a four- or five-star hotel and asking the concierge about the job. Most concierges are more than willing to talk about what they do, because they have a passion for the field. Consider studying hotel management in college, or at least getting a summer job as a bellhop.

INNSITTER

OVERVIEW

Ever think about who watches the inn when the inn's owners need a vacation of their own? Enter the innsitter, a kind of temporary inn owner, who can step in and run a bed-and-breakfast or inn so that the owners can take a deserved break without worrying about what's happening to their business.

Innsitters typically provide everything from food service to office communications, guest services, general property care, maintenance, housekeeping, and staff supervision to pet care and special requests. When the owner goes away for a break, the innsitter assumes the daily management of the property, and operates it without interruption in the unique style of service the owner has established. With consistency, continuity, and care, the innsitter ensures that the owner's business credibility is maintained as though you'd never left.

After all, the very nature of a B&B business doesn't really give an owner any freedom or time for travel, because they're busy meeting the needs of the guests.

Basically, an innsitter is a substitute innkeeper—the professionals that an innkeeper or bed-and-breakfast owner can call to step in and take over for a few days so the innkeeper can get away. Innsitters can be found around the world, just waiting for innkeepers to call them to come take over for a day or a week. During an emergency or when a break is required, the owner would have to close down the property or ask a friend or relative to help if it wasn't for the innsitter.

It may seem that innsitting is a simple, easy sort of part-time job, but nothing could

AT A GLANCE

Salary Range

Innsitters usually bill in 24-hour increments, with mileage extra, and the range typically runs from about $120 to $200 a day. Room cleaning can incur extra fees, depending on the number of rooms. The daily rate typically depends on how large the property is and the number of responsibilities expected. There is usually a higher rate during holidays and special events. Typically, an innsitter scheduled to work for at least two weeks may ask for half of the fee in advance.

Education/Experience

You can get a degree in hotel management from a four-year university, or take a more informal route and attend classes and seminars along with an apprenticeship at a bed-and-breakfast (more than one would be very helpful). There are also a number of innsitter associations that can provide helpful information (see Appendix A).

Personal Attributes

Innsitters must be gracious, adaptable, flexible, spontaneous, friendly, extremely organized, able to think on their feet, get along with staff, and be an effective crisis manager. An innkeeper needs to be personable, trustworthy, quick-thinking and -reacting, but most of all enjoy the company of others. Your day is filled with meeting the requests and needs of guests. Innkeeping is a professional position requiring a professional behavior and appearance.

Requirements

You've got to be able to be able to step in and handle the finances, the computer, the registrations, the meals, the staff, and the day-to-day business of running an inn. An innsitter must be able to prepare breakfasts with flair and cook with confidence and creativity, understand reservation systems software and email systems, and have a good phone manner. Innsitters must have excellent property and money management skills and come with top notch references.

Outlook

Innsitting is a growing field, with more and more opportunities.

Ken and Jo-Anne Garside, innsitters

The husband-and-wife team of Ken and Jo-Anne Garside offer a desirable "two for one" deal, bringing the team approach to the job, along with Ken's love of baking and cooking. Running Garside Innsitting Services, the Garsides offer owners affordable rates, flexible scheduling, current references, and a strong customer focus.

In the early 1990s, the couple explored the options of owning an inn, either building from scratch, buying one already established, or remodeling a home into a B&B. "The numbers just didn't show where a profit could be made until the sale of the inn," Ken says. "Most innkeepers have another income such as retirement, or full-time jobs, and the inn is a second income. We wanted to stay involved in the industry, so we looked at where we could fill a need for innkeepers."

The two realized that for innkeepers, getting time off or finding help in an emergency was just about impossible. That's when the idea of innsitting came to them. "We were among a few pioneers in the field," Ken says. "Today, there are several people offering the service, some [of whom] we have trained in our classes."

The two have been running their business since 1994, and can handle anything from a small B&B to a midsized inn with dinner service. As innsitters, they've accompanied AAA and Mobil hotel inspectors, supervised renovations, and coordinated special events such as weddings and mystery weekends.

When they innsit, the Garsides also offer owners a "First Aid Kit" consulting package including an evaluation of the operation plus useful recommendations for improvement. This service is ideal for innkeepers looking for a rest from a flagging business that could use a boost.

"We enjoy the guests and preparing special breakfast dishes," Ken says. What they don't like are surprises—and that's what happens when the innkeepers fail to give them certain information when they list the innsitter duties. Then there's what they like to call "the Curse of the Innkeeper."

"The curse happens when we inquire how to deal with a certain situation and the innkeeper replies: 'That never happens.' We are then on alert, for we know something like that will occur while they are gone."

The two also offer innkeepers advice on preparing for a AAA inspection. "Preparing for a AAA inspection requires innkeepers to comply with specific standards," Ken says. "Some innkeepers find it difficult to take the time to organize and prepare the information required. This is where we are of assistance." The two prepare the necessary documents, list required items needed in the rooms, or services to be offered to guests, in order to meet the requirements for the various ratings. If necessary, the two can obtain these items and services. "We also communicate with AAA to clarify gray areas," they say. "All the innkeeper has to do is sign the papers and mail it in. If it is done well, AAA will forgo the on-site inspection. We became involved because innkeepers who were already meeting the standards were not taking advantage of the referral base AAA offers."

The problem comes when some innkeepers look for someone at the last minute. "Innkeepers have a tendency to undervalue all they do in the course of a day and night," Ken says. "Operating an inn is a 24-hour job. When someone outside the situation begins to put a dollar amount on the task and responsibility it is difficult for innkeepers to accept the totals."

The two charge a per-day fee based on the size of the inn and the room rates. (Rooms with higher rates usually require more attention from the innkeepers.) For any time worked over the 24 hours, such as the first and last partial days, an hourly fee is charged until the inn's service is returned to the innkeeper. In addition, a full day of orientation is necessary, and the innkeepers pay the two for this orientation day.

Any service required beyond taking reservations, checking guests in and out, breakfast service and concierge service during the day has additional charges—this might include cleaning, laundry, turndown, garden care, special events, and pet care (most inns have at least one pet).

be further from the truth. Innsitting is much harder than many individuals realize. In fact, it's much more work than running your own place, because you have to be able to do things someone else's way—not your own. Most likely there will be all sorts of things to learn about—systems, programs, styles of handling guests. The computer and security systems may be different, the kitchen may require a whole different set of skills. In a B&B, you may be required to provide the morning meal, and you'll need to follow the requirements of the owners, not your own tastes. This is why most innsitters are themselves experienced inn or B&B owners who have either retired or given up running their own place because of financial issues.

At smaller B&Bs the innsitter often does the laundry, housekeeping, and cooking chores by himself or herself. But for those properties with housekeeping or waitstaff, the innsitter supervises their work, ensuring that the owner's standards are maintained.

An innsitter means that the owners can go away knowing that their business will continue to be run just the way they would like. They don't have to worry about customer service, and the owner's pets can also be taken care of just as if they were home. Most innsitters are available throughout the year, including holidays.

These days, the trend is to refer to innsitters as "interim managers"—and you don't necessarily have to limit yourself to an inn or B&B. Some corporations need interim managers to fill in until a person is hired permanently or during the start-up of a new property. Interim management as a full time position requires a great deal

of travel and constant building of a client base, where you'll work as an independent contractor.

If the idea of innsitting interests you, you might start by learning the basic operations of an inn, the responsibilities of innkeeper, and state and local rules and regulations regarding lodging and sanitation. Getting a degree in hospitality at a local college can help. In larger cities, you can get experience as a desk clerk, which can serve as an entry-level job leading to a management position.

Pitfalls

It can be difficult to take over an existing business and run it effortlessly if it's all new to you. The hours can be killer, and while you put in the work, you don't have the satisfaction of running your own place. You'll also be bound to follow the rules of the owners, which may conflict with how you believe in running a business.

Perks

Being an innsitter can be a terrific way to satisfy your longing to run an inn without the financial outlay owning a B&B or inn requires. If you truly love the business, this can provide you with lots of independence, freedom, and a job that's always different.

Get a Jump on the Job

To find out what it takes to run an inn, you can start with a weekend or summer job at a small inn or B&B near your home. Even with the lowliest job available, this is the best training for finding out exactly what it takes to run a B&B or inn.

LOCKSMITH

OVERVIEW

At some point in their lives, most people need the services of a locksmith. They might come to the rescue and unlock the house for a customer who, running late for work, grabbed the coffee but forgot the keys sitting on the dresser. Or they might need to retrieve the keys locked in the car of a customer who set them down to grab the groceries or comfort a crying baby, and shut the door before grabbing them.

Once on the scene, the locksmith will assess the situation and determine the best solution to the problem; because each lock and each situation is different. However, before actually beginning the job, the locksmith needs to make sure that the person requesting services is the owner of the house, car, or storage unit—or at least is authorized to have the locksmith open whatever is locked. This is important for legal and liability reasons.

Although locksmiths are mostly closely associated with rescuing keys; their work isn't always heroic. Locksmiths also install locks on newly constructed houses, offices, and retail buildings. Apartment complexes, businesses, hotels, and motels often contract with a locksmith to change or rekey the locks each time a tenant or employee leaves, or when a guest fails to return a key at the end of the stay. These types of businesses may also have the locksmith change or re-key the locks from time to time for security purposes. The locksmith will then use a key-duplicating machine to provide keys to be given to the apartment tenants, business employees, or hotel/motel guests.

Locksmiths are also called upon to repair broken or jammed locks. To do so, the locksmith will disassemble the lock and examine

AT A GLANCE

Salary Range

Nationwide, the median salary for full-time locksmiths is close to $31,000, with half of all full-time locksmiths earning between $25,000 and $37,000.

Education/Experience

Employers may prefer to hire individuals with at least a high school diploma or GED. Locksmiths learn their trade in formal training programs or on-the-job training. Many locksmiths eventually open their own businesses, so classes in management, accounting, marketing, computers, and other business-related topics would be very helpful.

Personal Attributes

Locksmiths need to be honest and trustworthy, with good problem-solving skills as well as an understanding of how things work and how parts interact. Locksmiths should be patient, detail-oriented, and accurate in their work. Ability to read and comprehend technical materials and repair manuals is important, as is good vision and manual dexterity. Locksmiths need to be self-starters who are able to work well independently. They also need good social skills for dealing with customers.

Requirements

Requirements vary from city to city and state to state, but many places require locksmiths to be licensed. Licensing requirements may include a written examination, background check, and payment of a licensing fee. A criminal background may (but does not necessarily) exclude an applicant from becoming a locksmith. Locksmiths are usually required to be bonded and insured. Self-employed locksmiths will probably need to file Doing Business As (DBA) papers, secure a tax license, and acquire any other permits required under local and/or state ordinances.

Outlook

There are currently around 23,000 locksmiths employed nationwide. The outlook for new locksmiths is good with a faster than average growth rate expected through about 2012. Many of the new jobs will come from the construction of new homes and office buildings that will need locks and deadbolts installed.

Lewis Barber, master locksmith

When parents or grandparents own a business, it's not uncommon for the children to get involved at an early age. That was the case for Lewis Barber. He began his apprenticeship when he was 11, with his grandfather, a self-taught locksmith. "At 13," he says, "I graduated from a formal Associated Locksmiths of America apprenticeship, becoming the youngest person ever to do so." Today, Barber says he keeps up with all the latest advances in locksmithing by attending classes each year, usually offered through suppliers. He runs the family business that his grandfather opened in 1956.

In order to keep the business growing, Barber has had to diversify. Today, in addition to traditional locksmith services, the business offers a wide range of services ranging from installation and maintenance of keyless systems, the sale and repair of closed-circuit TV systems, safe opening and repair, steel door replacement, and more.

Over the years, Barber has seen many changes in the trade since he began, and he expects that the field will continue to experience drastic changes. "The locksmith of today will no longer be," he predicts. "By 2020, everything will be push button locks. There will be no more keys." This means that locksmiths of the future will need to have a strong knowledge of electronics.

"It takes a special type of person to do this job," he says. "A locksmith needs the mind of an engineer and the skill of a surgeon"—as well as master puzzle manipulators with excellent problem-solving skills. But to run a successful business, it's all about customer service, and Barber offers his customers 24/7 service.

"The worst part of the job is getting up at 2 a.m. in the winter to let someone into their house or car," admits Barber, who is a hands-on business owner. When his employees grumble about a job or a late night call, Barber reminds them that he doesn't have them doing anything that he's not out there doing himself.

But even those 2 a.m. wake-up calls from desperate customers don't quell Barber's enthusiasm for the job. He enjoys getting to travel and having the opportunity to meet new people every day; people he ordinarily might not have the chance to meet. "It's definitely not boring," he says. "It's a different job every day, and it always keeps me thinking." Barber also enjoys being his own boss.

If you're interested in becoming a locksmith, Barber suggests going to a larger city and apprenticing. "In a big city, there is always someone looking for an apprentice." But he warns that it will take two-and-a-half to three years to learn the skills. In addition, if you set up your own shop you'll need about $100,000 worth of equipment to get going, including the tools needed to take apart and work on the newer locks and the electronics.

To be successful, you need to be willing to diversify; you can't just offer locksmith services, and as Barber knows, you can't run a business if you aren't there; you have to be a hands-on owner. "But you can make it, if this is the thing for you and you're willing to give 110 percent or more to make it work."

Barber says that his eight-year-old son is interested in electronics—and he may be the next generation to carry on the family business. To learn more about Barber's family-owned business and the services that they offer, you can check out their Web site at http://www.gilboes.com.

its inner workings. The pieces will be cleaned and any broken or malfunctioning parts will be replaced. Although parts are usually available from the manufacturer, sometimes the locksmith needs to make a replacement part using a lathe, drill, grinder, or other tools. In addition to traditional key locks, some locksmiths sell, install, and service electronic alarms and surveillance systems. Some locksmiths also sell and repair safes and vaults.

There are two ways someone learns the skills required of a locksmith: on-the-job-training or a formal locksmith training program. There are three types of locksmithing programs: through the mail via a correspondence course, *resident* (classes at a school), or *traveling resident* (classes at a sponsored site). There are several dozen schools throughout the United States that offer locksmith training taking several months to several years to complete, depending on the school and any specialties the student chooses.

Once you learn how to be a locksmith, several professional associations offer various levels of certification. Earning those certifications usually involves completing additional training and/or passing proficiency exams. Locksmiths keep up on the latest advances in their field by attending continuing education seminars and classes from lock manufacturers, locksmithing schools, and professional locksmith organizations. A yearly convention, sponsored by the Associated Locksmiths of America (ALOA), offers locksmiths the opportunity to take classes, network, and check out all that's new in locks and security by visiting ALOA's Security Expo.

Most locksmiths work for small businesses; some eventually open their own businesses. However, some locksmiths also work for universities, hospitals, city governments, and other large companies and corporations.

Pitfalls

Many locksmiths need to be on call nights, weekends, and holidays, to deal with customer emergencies. A locksmith working for someone else may end up having to do a lot of the late night or weekend calls. Locksmiths often work alone, with little interaction with other locksmiths or customers. Self-employed locksmiths need to provide benefits for themselves and anyone they employ.

Perks

Self-employed locksmiths can set their own hours, and can schedule vacations when they want. Locksmiths sometimes meet a variety of interesting individuals while working on a job.

Get a Jump on the Job

While in high school, take as many practical, trade-related classes as possible, including drafting, machining, metalworking, mechanics, introduction to business, and industrial and technology classes. Math and English classes are also important. If you're interested in working with electronic alarms and surveillance systems, an understanding of electronics and electricity is needed. If possible, look for a job working in a locksmith shop during school vacations. Start to learn the language (a locksmith dictionary can be found at http://www.locksoft.com/gloscopy.htm). If you're seriously interested in becoming a locksmith, you may be able to start a correspondence program while still in high school.

MATCHMAKER

OVERVIEW

Alicia Silverstone gave it a go as a full-time divorce lawyer turned part-time matchmaker in the short-lived series, *Miss Match*. Barbara Streisand shone in *Hello, Dolly!* as the incomparable Dolly Levi, looking not only to match up others, but herself as well. Perhaps the most famous movie matchmaker is that of Yente in *Fiddler on the Roof*. But do people outside of the movies and TV series really use matchmakers to "find them the perfect match"? You bet. Matchmaking was a $600 million industry in 2001. If you enjoy fixing up your friends, matchmaking might be the perfect career for you.

Working as a matchmaker is as interesting, exciting, and fun as it sounds, but it's also a lot of hard work. Everywhere the successful matchmaker goes, from the laundromat to the post office, there's networking to be done—talking to everyone about the matchmaking business, uncovering new clients, or searching for the perfect match for people already in the company's database. Networking and word-of-mouth from happy customers are two of the best ways to build a successful matchmaking business—and they're free.

When a new client comes into the office, the matchmaker will interview the person to learn what he or she is looking for. Before actually adding the new client to the company's database, the matchmaker may do a bit of detective work to verify that the information the client has given is accurate—things such as name, address, marital status, and criminal history. Your reputation as matchmaker can make or break your business, and screening potential

AT A GLANCE

Salary Range

The average matchmaker earns $20,000 to $100,000 or more per year. The amount depends on a number of factors, including the matchmaker's geographic location, the clientele, and the number of clients in the matchmaker's database. As with many other businesses, the salary also depends on how much time and energy the matchmaker puts into making the business a success.

Education/Experience

None required. Matchmaker Institute offers certification through a training program that has been approved by the New York State Education Department. Computer skills, especially understanding and using databases, are important. Many matchmakers are self-employed, so classes in accounting, marketing, public relations, and other business-related topics would be very helpful.

Personal Attributes

Matchmakers need to be very social with great people skills. They need to be friendly and upbeat and enjoy meeting and learning about new people. Matchmakers need to be good listeners who people tend to trust, and they need to be able to "read" people. They need a good sense of intuition, good communication skills, and patience. Matchmakers also need to be hardworking self-starters who are willing to talk to anyone and everyone they meet about their business to build a large enough client database to be able to make matches. And, matchmakers need to love working with people and making them happy.

Requirements

None. However, self-employed matchmakers will probably need to file Doing Business As (DBA) papers and acquire any other local permits required under local and/or state ordinances.

Outlook

The matchmaking industry experienced a 300 percent growth from 1999 to 2003. Right now, matchmaking is one of the fastest growing service industries, growing in demand each year. And while it's hard to predict the exact future of matchmaking, one thing that's for sure is that there will always be singles looking for love.

Lisa Clampitt, matchmaker

I wanted to work with people and contribute to happiness in people's lives," Lisa Clampitt explains, so she started out pursuing a career as a social worker. But like many people, she struggled with what to do with her life and career. To make it worse, she was finding social work depressing. Finally, after 12 years as a social worker, she decided to change careers.

Clampitt did what most people do when they need a job: she began scouring the want ads. When she came across an ad for a matchmaker/dating service, Clampitt thought it might be the perfect job for her. "It was something I already loved to do. I was always setting up my single friends."

Little did Clampitt know when she answered that ad that she would draw on knowledge from her social work background. "The people skills really helped," she says. Clampitt went on to work for two matchmakers before setting out on her own.

"Matchmaking is an amazing job," Clampitt explains. She enjoys working with clients, hearing their excited feedback after meeting someone new, meeting new people, getting to understand them, and sharing their struggles and success throughout the matchmaking process. "It's exciting to see their progress and watching them ultimately meet someone," she says. "There is nothing more exciting."

However, Clampitt warns that starting out is tough. It takes hard work to create a successful company with enough clients to earn an income. And of course, Clampitt says that at times you have to deal with unhappy, angry clients: people who think you didn't make a good match, people disappointed because the other person wasn't interested, and people stuck in bad dating patterns.

Clampitt thinks her very successful matchmaking business is the result of her background as a social worker and her passion for setting people up for that success. "But I spent a lot of money making mistakes in my own business." Realizing that there was no place for a fledgling matchmaker to go and learn the business, Clampitt and a partner set up the Matchmaking Institute, a school to train matchmakers, in 2003. Since then, more than 100 students from around the world have come to the Institute to take the 11-course, 22-hour weekend-intensive program, and earn their certification. Clampitt enjoys the opportunity to bring people together with similar interests because of its uniqueness.

The Institute is also working to standardize and give credibility to the industry through their training and a network of approved professional matchmakers. This is something that is important in an industry where the client has an emotional stake in the outcome, and they are putting their trust in the matchmaker to make their dreams of finding the perfect match come true.

As for the future, Clampitt says, "Matchmaking is growing and will continue to grow. It's a market that never dries out." More and more singles are choosing to focus on their careers and marry later in life, and when they do, they face a divorce rate of 50 percent. Clampitt feels that because of those factors, there is more need for a third party (the matchmaker) to help them prioritize. Besides that, she says, "people like the personal touch of a matchmaker."

For wannabe matchmakers, Clampitt advises that you think about what assets you have. "Do you enjoy working with people and networking? Are you a people person? Do you like to hear peoples' personal stories? Are you business-savvy? Are you a risk-taker? Would you enjoy working for someone else?"

(continues)

(continued)

If it seems like a good fit, Clampitt says, "It's one of the most ideal careers if someone fits [that] profile. It's phenomenal, and you can do whatever you want to do with it. Think outside the box. Network and find your niche."

Clampitt says many successful matchmakers incorporate their own personal interests into their business, setting up pet lovers, members of specific religions, and more. One matchmaker even matches clients based on their interest in nonprofit organizations. So be creative.

Clampitt also suggests getting a sense of the interest and need in your community. The more proactive singles there are in a community, the more likely they will be to hire a matchmaker, she says, adding, "Matchmakers are needed anywhere!"

applicants is one way help build that reputation. Many clients actually appreciate the fact that the matchmaker takes the time to do this legwork for them.

After accepting a new client, the matchmaker will go through the company's database looking for other clients who meet the specifications of the new client. To keep track of the company's clients, the matchmaker usually sets up a computerized database with detailed information about each client, so computer skills are very important. The matchmaker will continue looking for prospective matches until the client is happy. The number of matches per month and other details are usually spelled out in the terms of a contract signed by the client, which is usually for 6 to 12 months. Anything less than six months may not give the matchmaker enough time to make the perfect introduction.

Arranging the perfect match is, of course, the primary job of the matchmaker, but it's hardly the only job. Matchmakers often host parties for their clients. These events give the matchmakers' clients an opportunity to meet each other in a large social setting. Sometimes perfect matches are made at these events because some-

times what people think they want in their perfect mate isn't what they really want.

And since finding the perfect match can sometimes be a long and emotional process, while the matchmaker is looking for that perfect someone, the matchmaker will serve as a dating coach, personal cheerleader, and hand-holder if necessary. The matchmaker might even work through some role-playing exercises with a client to build confidence and improve dating techniques.

There are no educational requirements to become a matchmaker, but that doesn't mean you don't have to do your homework before setting up shop. The more you learn before hand, the more quickly you can work towards building a successful business. You need to decide if you want to run your business out of your home or if you want to rent an office space or storefront; there are pros and cons to each, so you need to decide what will work best for your situation. Then you need to find out what types of permits are needed in your local area to open a matchmaking business. If you don't have one, you'll need to purchase a computer system and database software.

Before you can hang out your shingle, you also need to learn as much as possible about the matchmaking side of the business—such as where and how to find potential clients. And you'll need to become an expert in public relations, advertising, and networking, finding what works best in your area. To keep your expenses down, you'll want to figure out free or cheap ways to get the word out. To help build your client database, you might offer special rates or some other gimmick. After all, you can't make matches with an empty database.

Before clients start coming through the door, you also need to develop interviewing and screening skills as well as matching techniques. How can you learn all this? You can learn a lot from reading everything you can find on matchmaking. Some matchmakers offer classes or workshops on how to become a matchmaker. You might have to travel for the class, or it may be done via e-mail, telephone, or correspondence. The Matchmaking Institute offers a training program that leads to certification.

Once your business is up and running, don't be surprised if you need to make one additional purchase—a new dress or suit. Successful matchmakers get invited to a lot of weddings.

Pitfalls

Running a matchmaking business is hard work. You will spend a lot of time doing the advertising, public relations, and networking needed to get your business going and keep it growing. Matchmakers often work long hours, especially when they are hosting an evening event or get-together. There is just no pleasing some people. Matchmakers will have to deal with very demanding customers, doing their best to make the client happy. It may be necessary to relocate to a different geographic location to build a successful business.

Perks

Matchmakers enjoy a flexible schedule with the opportunity to work from home (if they choose). They have the opportunity to meet and work with some very interesting people. It can be relatively inexpensive to open your own business. Matchmaking can be a career for life; you're never too old to help someone find the perfect mate. Matchmaking is the ultimate feel-good job, you truly have the chance to make people happy and change their lives

Get a Jump on the Job

Consider taking business and computer classes in high school or at a local junior or community college. Learn to design and use computer database systems. To keep your business up and running, learn some basic computer maintenance and repair so you can maintain your system. If possible, look for a job working for a matchmaking business during school vacations. Even if it's only answering phones or inputting information into the database you'll still get a little experience with this profession in the "real world."

MYSTERY SHOPPER

OVERVIEW

Imagine getting paid for going shopping, eating at your favorite restaurant, playing a round of golf, spending a day at an amusement park, or going on an all-expense paid cruise. Sound too good to be true? Well, with a lot of hard work and maybe just a little bit of luck, you can.

Anyone who works in any customer-oriented field knows that making the customers happy is important, because when customers aren't happy they take their business (along with their money) somewhere else. Small business owners can usually keep a close eye on their businesses and how their employees deal with their customers. But for franchises and other businesses with several locations and many more employees, it is much harder to keep tabs on the customer service. It would be costly for the business to hire someone to evaluate their service, so instead they work with companies who hire independent contractors to give them input on the things they are doing right, and what could use some work. And it isn't just retail shops and restaurants checking on their employees; banks, auto repair shops, health clubs, bowling alleys, roller skating rinks, and even government offices are just some of the places being evaluated.

The evaluator, usually known as a mystery or secret shopper, poses as an ordinary customer in order to secretly evaluate the customer service, cleanliness, and other details of an average shopping trip.

A shopper's job might start in the parking lot, after all it's the first and last impression the customer will have of the store. The shopper might comment on the number of shopping

AT A GLANCE

Salary Range

Most assignments, or "shops" as they are called in the industry, pay from $12 to $35. The average pay for a restaurant shop ranges from a free meal to $35. The average pay for a retail shop runs from $12 to $30. Bank and financial institution shops, which are more difficult to do, and require more extensive reporting, pay an average of $30 to $70. Some jobs also have perks like a service (maybe a free oil change, or a haircut), admission to an activity or event (bowling, an ice skating show, or the circus, for example), or a night at a hotel. Full-time mystery shoppers, can make $50,000 or more per year.

Education/Experience

Depends on the company, some require a high school diploma or GED. Certification and other training are available, but not required. Writing skills are very important, so classes in English and composition might be very helpful.

Personal Attributes

A good mystery shopper is detail-oriented and observant, with a good memory for names and other small details. They must be responsible and dependable. Mystery shoppers need to be able to follow directions. They need good, descriptive writing skills. Organizational skills are essential, as a mystery shopper has multiple forms, paperwork, and other details to keep track of for each job.

Requirements

Must be at least 18 years old for most job assignments. Specific assignments may have additional requirements depending on the job. For example, a shopper might need to own a home for a mortgage company assignment, or be of legal drinking age for a liquor store assignment. In Nevada, it is illegal for mystery shoppers to work as independent contractors. State law requires that they be employed by a private investigator.

(continues)

AT A GLANCE *(continued)*

Fines run $2,500 or more per offense. Florida has also passed legislation regarding mystery shopping. There are state laws around the country regulating the use of microphones and/or video cameras during an assignment (sometimes called a "video shop"). Mystery shoppers need to be aware of any local and state laws regarding their profession, and they need to stay up-to-date as new legislation is introduced and passed into law.

Outlook

Mystery shopping is a very competitive field. According to the Mystery Shopping Providers Association (MSPA), there are currently more than 200,000 mystery shoppers in the United States, with more people applying daily. Depending on the area, competition for jobs may be fierce.

carts around the lot, trash lying all around, or poor lighting (if it's at night).

Once inside the store, the shopper might time how long it takes an employee to greet her, or ask if the shopper needs help locating something. For accuracy, the shopper uses a digital watch to keep track of the time. The shopper will also note the name of the employee and how helpful he was; did he simply point the shopper in the general direction of the item she was looking for, or did he take her to it?

The shopper is sort of like a private eye, working undercover, so staying anonymous is important. The shopper can't exactly be jotting down notes, because employees may suspect they are being evaluated and they won't treat her like they would a typical customer. As some point the shopper might need to duck into the bathroom to jot down some notes. And, while she's in there, she might check out the condition of the bathroom.

Most shops require the shopper to make a small purchase so that she can evaluate the checkout process. The shopper will take note of the number of registers open, how long she has to wait in line, the speed and friendliness of the cashier, and the accuracy of the bill and her change. Once she is back in her car, the shopper will make notes about her entire shopping experience so that she can accurately complete her report.

Once the shopper is done for the day (some seasoned shoppers will schedule several jobs on the same day), she will fill out a questionnaire about the shop. Depending on the assignment, she may also have to prepare a written narrative describing her experiences. Most, if not all, the reports are filed via the Web, so reliable access to the Internet as well as some computer skills are important for a mystery shopper.

If you are interested in getting started as a mystery shopper, a quick Internet search on the keywords *mystery shopper* will return listings of places you can apply to become a mystery shopper. Once you start surfing around for more information, you'll find hundreds upon hundreds of companies claiming to be looking for mystery shoppers. Professionals usually recommend against applying with companies that charge an application fee. And, if something doesn't seem quite right, you can always check it out with the Better Business Bureau.

A great way to get information is to network with people who are already working as mystery shoppers. There are many online forums where you can find out who pays on time and who doesn't, the best places to apply, places to skip, tips for getting your first shop, and a whole lot more.

Once you have selected a few companies you'd like to shop for, you can apply right online. One of the things you will be

Niccole Rogers, mystery shopper

Mystery shopping is a huge, billion-dollar industry, but not too long ago all you had to do to break into the field was to network with the manager of a local store. That's exactly how Niccole Rogers got her start. "About 12 years ago, I started going into stores and speaking with the manager about their customer service," she says. In exchange, Rogers said she worked out a deal with the manager for perks or compensation if she'd continue to give feedback. "You can't do that anymore," she notes.

Today, mystery shopping is still a mystery to many people, but there are laws on the books mandating requirements for mystery shoppers and in some cases limiting what they can or can't do. Rogers explains that most mystery shopping assignments require the shopper to be at least 18 years old. "The majority of mystery shoppers are independent contractors, and individuals under the age of 18 can't enter into a legally binding contract." Among her credentials, Rogers is a licensed private investigator, a requirement of the state of Florida where she lives and works. "State laws change so much, it's really up to the independent contractor (shopper) to make sure that they are in compliance."

Today, Rogers runs the National Center for Professional Mystery Shoppers and Merchandisers (NCPMS), a national not-for-profit organization working to educate, empower, and support mystery shoppers. One of the many services offered by the NCPMS is training and certification.

Is training really necessary to learn to shop? Mystery shopping involves a lot more than simply shopping. The training will help someone learn to manage their contracts as well as manage the companies with which they work. Training will also help you to know what to look for when selecting an assignment, because believe it or not, it's actually possible you'll lose money on a shop when you factor in the taxes, gas, and more. "Certification will become a major player in the future in weeding out people without the experience and maturity to finish the job," she says.

Training will also help shoppers develop the right attitude. "People come in and want to do this, but they don't understand this is a job; it's work." Rogers says that while it's possible to have fun on the job, it's important to remember that people are counting on you to be responsible.

asked is the town or towns where you'd like to work. Remember the more towns you list, the more chances you'll have to work. You will also be asked to write about a shopping experience, maybe your best experience, your worst experience, or just a recent experience. Follow any directions you are given, and treat it as if it were a real job assignment. And be sure that your writing sample has no spelling or grammar errors.

Once you get your first assignment, get out there and do it and do it well. One

expert estimates that as many as 80 percent of new shoppers don't do the job at all. It is also estimated that 25 percent of jobs aren't completed correctly, so follow the directions. Remember, the better the job you do, the more likely you are to be chosen again.

After your first few assignments (or maybe even before you get started) you'll probably realize that there is a lot more to being a successful mystery shopper than simply doing the shop and filling out the questionnaire. Several companies offer cer-

You'd think that the perks, as well as just getting paid to shop, would be the greatest part of the job, but not for Rogers. She loves the reporting or summary part of the job. "Great customer service is hard to find," she says. "When someone does their job well, simply because it's their job, and you can recognize and reward them [in your report], that's awesome!" Of course even the best of jobs has at least one downside. With mystery shopping, the biggest negative is the time you have to wait to get paid; it can take four to six weeks or longer to get paid, and if you were required to make a purchase, your credit card can start to rack up interest.

For someone interested in becoming a mystery shopper, Rogers says there are three rules. "You must love to shop and like being at the store all the time. You need a great eye for detail. And you need to be great at writing and managing paperwork. If you can do those three things and you want to be a mystery shopper, more than likely you can succeed.

For someone just starting out, Rogers advises that you start slow. "It pays to get your feet wet by getting some experience with lower paying jobs." She also says it's important to understand the assignment. "Read the instructions. The details on some assignments can be very specific, down to what time to be in a certain area of the store. If you don't complete the assignment correctly or completely [as directed], they don't have to pay you."

What about the e-mails and Web sites that promise mystery shopping jobs for a fee? "Bottom line, you should not pay for an assignment," she says. "You shouldn't pay someone to work." But she adds that there are times it's helpful to pay for information. Her advice? Ask yourself, "What is it you're paying for? Is it worth it to you? How is this information going to help you?"

If mystery shopping still sounds like the job for you, Rogers says, "Don't let the number [of other mystery shoppers] scare you off." You hear a lot of large numbers, but Rogers says you need to look at what the numbers are really telling you. How many of those are active shoppers? If people register and never do a shop, or do it one time, that doesn't make them a mystery shopper. And remember, there is a high turnover rate.

tification to help you learn the ins and outs of mystery shopping. The certification programs are usually under $100. Some are online courses while others are in-person workshops. With the different options that are available, you can choose the one that best meets your needs.

There are also several conventions each year for mystery shoppers. These conventions offer workshops and classes to help the serious shopper learn and maybe get an edge over the competition. Conventions are also a great way to network and meet face-to-face with other shoppers, which is nice, because being a mystery shopper is a solitary profession.

It's a long road from shopping your local gas station or fast good restaurant to an all-expense paid Caribbean cruise; but if you're willing to work hard, do the job, and do it well, you might just make it.

Pitfalls

With all the competition, it can be tough to break into mystery shopping and get the choice assignments. It takes a lot of time and effort to make a full-time living. And, since mystery shoppers work as independent contractors, they need to provide their own benefits like health insurance and retirement savings.

Perks

Mystery shoppers can set their own hours by picking and choosing assignments that fit with their schedules. And, since they can choose their own assignments, shoppers can work as much or as little as they like.

Some shoppers with small children like that they can take their kids to work with them. Some shoppers "work" on vacation, scheduling hotel and restaurant shops in their vacation destinations.

Get a Jump on the Job

Students interested in a career in mystery shopping can work on their descriptive writing skills. Students serious about it might consider working on one or more of the certifications available.

NANNY

OVERVIEW

The modern-day nanny is a mixture of Mary Poppins and high-tech household manager, and with the right mix, the person can earn a very healthy salary and a lot of self-respect. If the thought of diapering an infant while watching a toddler and supervising an elementary school child doesn't curl your hair, you may have what it takes to be a nanny—someone hired by a family to take care of their children.

Nannies usually take care of children from birth to age 10 or 12, tending to the child's early education, nutrition, health, and other needs. Nannies may either live full time with the family or simply drive to the home each day, but in either case, duties are typically centered on child care and any domestic tasks related to child care, not household duties or cooking. This means you may make a child's lunch, but you won't be called on to cater a dinner party for 12. You'll make more money as a nanny than you will in any other career involving children—but that's because you'll be held responsible for the social, emotional, and intellectual development of the kids.

Modern-day America being what it is, nannies must have safety as the top priority at all times while taking care of the kids. Daily reading to the kids is essential, as is providing stimulating and educational play, crafts, and other activities. At the same time, the nanny must be a good model, watching her language and practicing healthy eating habits. Many families appreciate a "nanny log" in which the nanny keeps track of helpful information and details.

So what's a day in the life of a nanny look like? If you live with the family, you'll

AT A GLANCE

Salary Range

Salary varies widely according to location, with highest salaries in large cities such as New York, Washington, D.C., Boston, and Los Angeles, according to the International Nanny Association salary survey. In addition, nannies typically expect paid holidays and two weeks paid vacation, usually timed to coincide with family vacation schedules. Sick day arrangements vary. Live-in nannies get free room and board. Typical benefits include annual bonus, jewelry, gift certificates, cameras, spa trips, movie and theater tickets, DVDs, VCRs, and coverage of any nanny-related conference expenses.

Education/Experience

While a specific educational program is not required, any sort of child-rearing education or classes will be helpful, as are safety certifications such as CPR or Red Cross safety or first aid classes. Some nannies complete special nanny programs. Schools for nannies teach early childhood education, nutrition, and child care. Others have degrees in early childhood education, developmental psychology, or human development. Some employers prefer to hire nannies with secondary or postsecondary courses in child development and early childhood education, or work experience in a child care setting. Other employers require their own specialized training. An increasing number of employers require an associate degree in early childhood education.

Personal Attributes

You must be dependable, adaptable, responsible, flexible, patient, honest—and love children. In addition, nannies must be self-starters with lots of initiative who can organize the day to get everything done. A nanny must also be a good communicator with the patience to listen to children for many hours at a time and yet let the family know when there are problems in a calm, professional manner. Child-care workers must

(continues)

AT A GLANCE *(continued)*

anticipate and prevent problems, deal with disruptive children, provide fair but firm discipline, and be enthusiastic and constantly alert. They must communicate effectively with the children and their parents, as well as other teachers and child-care workers. Workers should be mature, patient, understanding, and articulate, and have energy and physical stamina. Skills in music, art, drama, and storytelling are also important. Self-employed child-care workers must have business sense and management abilities.

Requirements

Most families require a criminal background check, solid references, and U.S. work authorization, as well as a driver's license, since you may need to drive the children to play dates, the doctor's office, or to school. (Nannies who don't drive will have more luck finding a job in a major metropolitan area with established public transit, such as New York City). The International Nanny Association offers a credential exam—a 90-minute multiple choice exam that measures a nanny's working knowledge in child development, communication, child guidance, diversity awareness, learning environment, personal qualities, safety, management skills, nutrition, and professionalism. The exam was written by leading child care experts and is a tangible way for nannies to prove themselves as professionals. Because the exam is challenging, it's strongly recommended that anyone sitting for the exam complete at least 2000 hours of professional child-care experience and obtain current certification in infant/child CPR and first aid.

Outlook

Qualified people who are interested in working as a nanny should have little trouble finding and keeping a job, since demand far outstrips supply. Opportunities for nannies should be especially good, as many workers prefer not to work in other people's homes.

the little ones. You may be expected to get the children up and serve them breakfast. You'll want to avoid watching TV all day, and you don't want to be plopping them in front of the TV so you have time to paint your nails, either. You shouldn't be chatting on the phone during work, and of course there's no smoking, drinking alcoholic beverages, using drugs, or swearing while on duty. Physical discipline is also strictly ruled out. You'll usually be expected to work from 8 to 10 hours a day, and you'll usually need to promise to work for at least a year for the family. You'll be working with the children in language development, potty training, manners, and homework. If they're in school, you'll need to make sure they get on the bus or get to school on time, and you'll be responsible for driving them to any activities after school.

Nannies find positions either through a nanny agency or via an online nanny agency. Nanny agencies typically prescreen applicants and forward to the client family only those nannies who meet the agency's criteria. This means that a prospective nanny must interview with the nanny agency, provide references, wait for the agency to check the references, and then wait for the agency to refer them to a specific family for an interview. Online agencies are typically more direct. They do not usually prescreen applicants; instead, the families are given interview forms and reference checking forms.

Although nannies spend most of their day working with children, they do maintain contact with parents or guardians through informal meetings or scheduled conferences to discuss each child's progress and needs. Many nannies (especially those who don't live with the family) keep records of each child's progress and suggest how parents can stimulate their child's learning and development themselves.

need to get yourself up and ready on your own, and if you live out, you need to be prompt and on time each and every day. As soon as you arrive, you'll be in charge of

Donna Robinson, The Traveling Nanny

As The Traveling Nanny, Donna Robinson brings professional child care to individual families all over the country. She is willing to travel to your location on a temporary nanny assignment, and can help parents choose a full-time nanny.

"I like the fact that I don't really have a box," she says. "I'm in charge and I can implement things I can also find a better way to do things. Always change and grow and be creative. How I do my job is going to affect the next generation. I can leave my stamp on the future . . . It's one of the most powerful jobs there is. I like being nurtured and nurturing others; it fulfills a great need to be nurturing and loving."

Robinson was 26 when she started work as a teacher assistant for a third grade class in California. She ran the creative writing center and worked with children who had behavior problems. "I'd always worked in business previously and it was the first time I realized that I loved working with children," she says. After a variety of corporate jobs and volunteer work with children, she began taking care of children as a long-term nanny. When her last long-term job with a family ended in 2001, she took some time to think about her talents and how to keep the nanny job fun. When she stumbled on a nanny classified Web site one day, she began to read parents' ads and realized how many parents needed a nanny within two weeks or less. "Having been a working parent, I recognized that panic and stressful feeling," she says. Realizing that one of her strengths was the ability to bond quickly with children and parents, and knowing that she enjoyed traveling, it seemed only logical to become a Traveling Nanny. "The fact there didn't seem to 'be such a thing' didn't discourage me," she says. "I have never looked back or regretted my choice."

A temporary nanny is used in many ways. Temporary nannies fill the gap when a family is between nannies or the regular nanny goes on vacation. If parents are especially busy at work for a brief period, a temporary nanny can step in and fill the void. During school vacations, a nanny can come and stay with the children for a month or two. Robinson also works as a "transitional nanny"—a form of temporary nanny. A transitional nanny steps in and cares for children when the family is hiring a new nanny. This gives parents a chance to find the right nanny without having to rush and search under stress of deadlines.

"I didn't become a nanny until I was 45, but I'd always worked with kids, all my life," she explains. "The thing that attracted me to the field is that I loved working with children. But what is very important is that you must love parents just as much. I have a great compassion for working parents and what they are trying to do for their kids."

Nannies in general often have negative experiences, she points out. "Typically, parents treat you as a servant and won't work with you as a team. Some parents can be very demanding. Personally, I've loved all my clients, although I've spent a lot of time mentoring parents."

The biggest enemy of the job is burnout, she says, when nannies work too many hours with no support. "The negative parts can be difficult if you're not careful or you're not an advocate for yourself," Robinson says. "Live-in nannies can be taken advantage of. Even if it's their day off, a parent might say 'Oh, are you going to be around?' Nannies tend to be very good at the child care part, but not so good at advocating for themselves."

(continues)

(continued)

But odds are, you've probably not heard too much about a career as a nanny. "No one ever gave a young person a Career Day talk about being a nanny," she says. It's a wonderful job for anyone who loves children and who is very creative. "Being a nanny is a real profession, and today you'll find more and more classes about how to be a nanny. If you're interested in being a nanny, I'd suggest getting all the babysitting experience you can, go to a junior college and take child care classes. You don't have to sign up for a degree."

She also recommends attending an International Nanny Association (INA) convention. "Listen to other nannies and learn," she says. "Experience is the best teacher. This is a profession. INA has a mentoring board, and they'll match you with someone who can help guide you."

The most important attribute for a nanny is nurturing ability. "Taking care of children is the greatest career for creative people," she says. "I became a nanny by accident. I stayed in it because it used all my talents, all the time, plus it fulfilled my need to nurture."

Pitfalls

It's not easy having total responsibility for kids for most of the day—especially if those kids aren't yours. The hours can be long and irregular; most nannies work at least 45 to 50 hours a week, and although nannies typically receive two consecutive days off a week, they may not always be Saturday and Sunday. Because some parent jobs have odd schedules (especially airline pilots, realtors, or physicians) you'll need to match your time to the parent's schedule. Live-in nannies usually work longer hours than do those who have their own homes, although if they work evenings or weekends, they may get other time off.

Perks

Being a nanny is hard work, but it's very rewarding. Nannies usually work in the pleasant and comfortable homes or apartments of employers wealthy enough to afford them. Most are day workers who live in their own homes and travel to work, although some live in the home of their employer, generally with their own room and bath. They often become part of their employer's family, and may derive satisfaction from caring for them. Most nannies also travel with the family during vacations, and therefore may see interesting parts of the world they may not otherwise have gotten the chance to visit. If the family is high powered or well known, the nanny may get to meet interesting, exciting people in the course of their duties, and make good contacts for future career moves. Watching children grow, learn, and gain new skills is also very rewarding.

Get a Jump on the Job

One of the best ways to prepare for a career as a nanny is to work now as a babysitter. The more families and children you can work with, the more you'll learn about child care and dealing with families. Take a course in babysitting that may be offered by your local Red Cross or high school, and volunteer at a day care or child care center for extra experience. Consider studying as much as you can about developmental psychology and infant and child care, and consider a major in early elementary education in college.

PAGEANT CONSULTANT

OVERVIEW

Beauty queens don't learn how to walk, pose, interview, and sparkle up on stage all by themselves. Because pageants are big business these days, you can't just wake up one day in a little town in Georgia and decide to go all the way to Atlantic City and capture a national crown. Today's participants require the intense services of a pageant coach to even hope to compete against some of the nation's most attractive and talented young women.

A beauty pageant coach's job starts with a serious discussion with a prospective beauty queen about her past competitions, and includes a review of the client's videos and resume. If the consultant thinks the client has potential, the two work out a plan to prepare for the next pageant deadline. This will usually include discussions about wardrobe, beauty, talent, and interview skills. Pageant consultants also work with clients on preparation of applications and paperwork, stage presence and confidence.

Pageant coaches typically provide a coaching "package" depending on the type of pageant a girl or young woman wants to enter and the amount of help required. Consultants typically offer advice by the hour, several-hour package, or weekend package. A weekend training session might include hours of intense interview training, including mock interviews, mental conditioning, application suggestions, how to walk in a gown, making a good first impression, how to handle onstage questions, platform preparation (for the Miss Ameri-

ca pageant), hair and makeup recommendations, a wardrobe analysis and shopping trip to an exclusive pageant store. For pageants that require talent, pageant consultants also work with clients on their talent presentation.

Just as in a college application, what you say and how you say it on your pageant application can have a big impact on how you're perceived. This paperwork will help the judges form questions to ask the contestant in the interview, and carries an

Connie Wallace, pageant consultant

The daughter of a state Mrs. America title holder, Connie Wallace grew up amidst the glitz and glamour of the pageant business, and she knew early on what she wanted to do. "I went everyplace with my mother," she recalls, "and her best friend ran the state Miss USA Pageant. She was like my aunt. I really grew up in the business."

Before long, she began participating in pageants herself, winning the Miss America Preliminary Title Holder; Miss Rhode Island World, Mrs. Rhode Island (America), and Mrs. New Jersey (United States). She's also hosted dozens of pageants and fashion shows throughout the Mid-Atlantic and New England, and she's also appeared in many local, regional, and national TV commercials and has co-hosted infomercials.

As the CEO/president of Crowning Achievements, a pageant consultant company, she offers individualized coaching and consulting services for pageant participants aged 16 and up. Her daughters are also active in the business. "They've been around pageants all their lives," she says. "They were helping with production and choreography since they were 12."

She can help participants with all phases of competition for all kinds of pageants, including tips on wardrobe, interview, walking, makeup, hair, talent, interviews, and photography. An individual coaching session might include a mock interview, wardrobe analysis and selection, personal appearance analysis, hair and makeup analysis, talent review, platform development, and consultation in speech and diction. For participants who live too far away, she also provides telephone advice and coaching.

"I like being able to give the girls self esteem," she says. "That's really what the pageants are all about." She's careful to separate the mainstream traditional beauty pageants that she handles from the "glitz pageants" of young children, which she does not. "The two are really quite different," she explains.

If you're interested in becoming a beauty pageant consultant, you're probably already involved in pageants in some fashion. There really isn't a standard educational path to becoming a consultant—what it takes is old-fashioned hard work and experience in pageants themselves. "You need experience in competing," she says, "and in every other aspect of the pageant. I've been a director, coordinator, backstage helper—I've worked in every capacity. This experience develops your eye and helps you understand what you need to be successful. It takes years to get that experience."

Growing up in the trade helps, she says. But if you're not from a pageant family, you can help out at pageants and get an internship in a pageant consultant office to really see what goes on behind the scenes.

Participating in a couple of pageants and then deciding you want to be a consultant just isn't enough, she explains. "You need to be totally familiar with all of the suppliers of the special products, the wardrobe, hair products—it's a whole other world, and it's very specific. For example, you need a special swimsuit to participate in a swimsuit competition—the kind of swimsuit you need would never actually be used in the water."

It's a business she loves and that's always different, but there's a downside, of course. "I don't like seeing the girls disappointed," she says. "But they learn from that. Winning gives you confidence, but losing gives you character."

impression of the contestant's accomplishments, goals, and level of preparedness. The consultant helps her clients fill out pageant applications using strategies that will prompt the judges to ask the questions she feels most confident answering. Together, consultant and client craft an application to showcase her achievements and help her application stand out from the rest.

The most important part of many pageants is the interview, so consultants typically spend a lot of time working with clients on this area. Even if the interview doesn't carry a lot of weight in the final score, the impression a contestant makes during the interview can affect her score in all other phases of competition. Whether the interview is a 10-minute session with a panel of judges or quick one-on-one interviews with separate judges, the consultant can teach her client the skills to control the interview and leave the judges wanting more. The consultant will offer advice on how to handle specific interview questions, mock interview situations, and onstage interviews. They will also give advice on how to create a lasting impression, what to wear for interviews, and what kind of hair and makeup works well in these situations.

Having the right look is obviously imperative, and so the typical pageant consultant spends a lot of time with clients on this aspect of competition, working on a client's walk, look, and confidence level. Choosing the right clothes depends on knowing the right look for the pageant system in which the client is competing. Consultants will help the client learn how to highlight her best assets and minimize those minor flaws she doesn't want noticed. She'll also discuss trends in hair and makeup, and hairstyles that work for each phase of competition. The consultant helps the client find a "total look" that best suits her personality and makes people notice her.

Most beauty pageants are all about the swimsuit, and so the pageant consultant will help her client discover what swimsuit flatters her body type and helps focus attention on her best qualities and downplays flaws. The consultant also helps the client select the right color for her skin tone, how to walk and pose during a swimsuit competition, and—if necessary—how to choose a personal trainer to help her get into top physical condition.

There's a lot of psychology in many pageants, and the consultant will help her client appear confident, knowledgeable, and in control by being mentally prepared for each phase of competition. The consultant can help her client harness the excitement and control the nerves, channeling that energy into preparing for any question or situation. While contestants can't predict what the judges will ask, they can learn to think on their feet and control the focus of an interview.

Finally, in many pageants talent is also important. Beauty pageant consultants, who are usually experienced in performing arts, can help a client improve her performance so as to make an emotional connection with the judges and the audience. Talent is judged not just on technique and ability but also on stage presence and entertainment value, so the consultant will work on all these areas, as well as costuming, song or music choice, and stage presence. If necessary, the consultant can arrange for additional coaching by experts in the client's particular talent area.

Pitfalls

There can be a great deal of stress in coaching beauty pageant contestants, which may involve travel to other states and endless travel on nights and weekends. In addition, pageant consultants are self-employed entrepreneurs, which means no benefits, no paid vacations or sick leave, and plenty of pressure to continually grow the business in order to ensure cash flow.

Perks

Most consultants were once beauty pageant contestants themselves, and truly love the whole experience of pageant work. They enjoy working with young women in coaching them to aim for success.

Get a Jump on the Job

Because pageant consultants were once contestants themselves, you should be attending as many pageants yourself as possible. Spend time as well polishing your talents and learning as much as possible about makeup, hair, wardrobes, and performing.

PERSONAL SHOPPER

OVERVIEW

Imagine a job where getting up and going to work means heading off to a major department store or specialty boutique and shopping, shopping, shopping; putting together fabulous outfits and picking out terrific gifts. Sounds too good to be true? Well, there is one catch: all the fruits of your shopping labors are for someone else.

Shopping may be one of America's favorite pastimes, but, believe it or not, there are people who don't have the time or desire to spend an afternoon at the mall searching for the perfect suit, blouse, shoes, or gift. As a result, many of the nation's top department stores, such as Macy's, Neiman Marcus, Bloomingdale's, Marshall Field's, and Saks Fifth Avenue, offer personal shopping services to their customers. Personal shopping isn't just a service and convenience for the customer, but it's beneficial for the store as well. It keeps the customers happy, and keeps them coming back for more, thereby increasing the retailer's profits.

For customers, it's as easy as calling the store or sending an e-mail to let a personal shopper know what items they are looking to buy. If a customer frequently uses the personal shopping services at particular stores, he or she will probably get to know one personal shopper who knows his or her tastes, likes, dislikes, needs, and budget. In fact, over time, a personal shopper might get to know the tastes and needs of the client so well that the shopper will put aside an item for the client that he or

Salary Range

Nationwide, the median salary for full-time personal shoppers working for large department stores is around $30,000, with half of all full-time personal shoppers earning between $22,000 and $37,000. Some department store personal shoppers work on commission which can drastically affect earnings, both good and bad. Some independent personal shoppers earn as much as $100,000 or more a year.

Education/Experience

No experience is required. A background in fashion and retail (gained in the classroom and/or through on-the-job training) will be helpful. For independent, self-employed personal shoppers, classes in management, accounting, marketing, and other business-related topics might be very useful.

Personal Attributes

Personal shoppers should be self-confident, organized people. They should enjoy working with and helping others. They need to be friendly and enthusiastic, but at the same time, not pushy. They need excellent listening and communication skills. They need to be patient while dealing with customers, and tactful in letting clients know that something that looked great on the hanger doesn't necessarily look great on them. Personal shoppers need to be customer-oriented with good people skills.

Requirements

Independent, self-employed shoppers will most likely need to file Doing Business As (DBA) papers, get a tax license, and acquire any other permits required under local and/or state ordinances. They may also be required to carry insurance and be bonded.

Outlook

It is hard to predict the exact outlook for personal shoppers. It appears that the demand for personal shoppers is growing, but since the business is so closely related to the retail industry, it may be negatively affected by adverse economic conditions. Competition for personal shopper jobs is generally very stiff.

Lori Johnson, personal shopper and certified image consultant

Like most children, Lori Johnson had a dream. "Ever since I was a little girl, it was my goal to help support women and make them feel better about themselves," she says. After graduating from high school, Johnson spent 17 years in several very diverse fields. In addition to earning a college degree in architectural design, Johnson held jobs in the retail apparel industry and the restaurant and hotel industries, as well as working in engineering design and even construction management. The time she spent in these seemingly unrelated industries were actually leading her to be able to fulfill that childhood dream by laying the groundwork for her to eventually open her imaging consulting business.

Johnson says that all those ventures gave her the "background tools" to succeed in her current business. "I incorporate all the experiences I have had into my work every day," she says. Her architectural design background taught her about design and color theory. While working at a full-service women's clothing shop, Johnson learned many of the things that would help her in her career as an image consultant and personal shopper. "I worked with the tailor and learned how alterations were done. I learned about the different designers, their styles and line. And I learned who fit [in terms of designers] and how to fit," she says.

But it was her experiences in the engineering world that would have the most impact on her future. She became a manager and was in a position where she was working primarily with older men. In order to be taken seriously, Johnson says, "I needed to create a positive image so that I could make a good first impression." In order to create that image Johnson read books and took classes. She studied everything from cosmetic application to etiquette to public speaking. Johnson continued to learn all she could by reading everything she could find about fabric, color, analysis, body style, figure-typing, and skin tone analysis. She took classes, grabbing any training she could find. After speaking at a local professional association, several individuals hired Johnson. For several years, she kept her "day job," offering consulting and shopping services parttime. Now Johnson is a full-time image consultant and personal shopper.

Johnson's clients are primarily corporate women. "I know where they are coming from, what they are looking for, and what they need." Johnson says image is important. "First impressions make a difference, and your appearance will open doors. You need that appearance going in or the door will shut and you'll lose that opportunity, whether it be a job interview, a sales call, a relationship, or a PTA meeting."

she might like, even if the client hasn't requested it.

Of course it takes time to get to that level with the customer. During the initial contact, the shopper will get some basic information about what the customer is looking for, getting as much specific information as possible, including an idea of the budget that the client is working with, so that the shopper can make informed decisions. Based on the wants and needs of the customer, the shopper will select a variety of items that meet the given criteria. The customer might come into the store to view the items. Many stores offer courier services so that customers can examine the items from the comfort of their homes or offices. If none of the items meet with the customer's approval, the shopper will work with the customer to find the perfect items, no matter if it's a bottle of perfume, a tie, a pair of socks, or a winter coat.

Even as important as first impressions are, Johnson says it's hard to get people to pay for her services. "No one is going to look me up in the yellow pages," she says. So she spends a big chunk of her time running the business end of her business, writing articles on the subject, doing media interviews, and networking. She is also an active member of many professional organizations. The president of the Association of Image Consultants International, New England chapter, she was voted member of the year in 2000 and again in 2005 for her commitment to the organization. Johnson also chairs the Ambassador's Group for the South Shore Chamber of Commerce.

Johnson admits that she makes less money now than she did in her engineering days. "But I am much happier," she says, "when I help somebody and see that look on their face that this is building self-esteem and knowing that they feel good about how they look." Johnson uses her talents outside the workplace as well. She is the founder of "Women of Influence," a nonprofit organization that assists less fortunate women.

Johnson says that image consulting and personal shopping is a fantastic opportunity. "There is plenty of room for more people in the field. It's a service that will always be in need. It's not going away."

And as fun as it sounds working with clients and shopping all day, Johnson says that it's important to understand that you have to make money to stay in business. "You need good business skills," she says. Realizing how important those skills would be to her success, Johnson went back to school to earn a two-year degree in business administration. "You have to be able to understand marketing, sales, accounting, bookkeeping, how to manage money, how to set up a budget, and how to set goals." And even though she runs a successful business, Johnson admits, "I hate the bookkeeping."

Johnson says that, for her, everything just came together. "There is no science or rules to this. You learn the basics and then add your own talents and gifts." Her job, she says, is very rewarding. "People are putting something very personal [their self-image] into my hands, and I take that very seriously."

To learn more about the services Johnson offers, see her portfolio, pick up some image tips, or sign up for her newsletter, visit her Web site at http://www.yourbestimagepid.com.

Personal shopping services offered by the upscale department stores and boutiques are probably most familiar to the general public, but that is just the tip of the personal shopping iceberg. There are many, many other possibilities for someone interested in becoming a personal shopper.

Some personal shoppers work for large corporations as corporate gift buyers. Gift giving is a huge part of the public relations at many large companies. Most corporate executives don't have the time or desire to deal with details of purchasing these gifts, so they hire an expert to pick out exactly the right gift for the client or the occasion.

Other shoppers focus on shopping for large events, corporate events, fundraising dinners, weddings, and other events. These shoppers might work for an event planner, or they might be independent (or freelance) shoppers who are contracted by an event planner. They will do the leg-work for the event planner, finding plates, flatware, linens, and decorations that meet the client's specifications for the event. The event planner can then take the shopper's selections to the client, along with information comparing costs, for the client's final approval.

Many personal shoppers are independent or freelance shoppers, meaning that they don't work for a specific store or business, but they shop to meet the needs of specific customers who hire them. For these individuals, the sky's the limit. In the right geographic location and economy, they can carve out a niche for themselves, specializing in shopping for wines, jewelry, home furnishings, gifts, clothing, or just about anything their clients want. Of course, not every freelance shopper will be able to make a living providing specialized shopping services, and not every shopper wants to specialize. Personal shoppers become personal shoppers because they enjoy shopping, and many shoppers enjoy shopping for a variety of different items.

With a lot of hard work and some creative advertising, freelance shoppers can build a client base that will call upon the shopper to make purchases for them. They might do the grocery shopping for housebound senior citizens or busy working moms who would rather spend Saturday mornings at their children's sporting events. They might purchase work clothes for busy businesspeople who would rather not shop for themselves. They might shop for a husband needing the perfect gifts for an anniversary, holiday, or birthday.

For some, personal shopping is just one of the many services provided as an image consultant. In addition to simply putting together terrific outfits, image consultants offer additional services such as makeovers, lessons in etiquette and social skills, personal coaching, networking and interviewing skills, and much more.

There are several full-length books and e-manuals that will teach you the ins and outs of personal shopping, but no formal education or training is required to become a personal shopper.

One of the best things you can do to prepare for a job as a personal shopper is to get some experience in retail sales. Even if you can't get a job working in the type of store where you'd like to be a personal shopper, you will get invaluable experience learning about products, brands, trends, and maybe most importantly, how to deal with customers. In fact, some department store personal shoppers start out on the sales floor and work into a position as a personal shopper. Some of those department store shoppers take their knowledge and experience and open their own personal shopping service.

Another way to prepare for a career as a personal shopper is to keep up with the latest trends and be familiar with the types of products your clients might ask you to purchase. If you hope to specialize in fashion, learn about the dress codes for your customers' professions, and then keep up with the latest fashion items and trends that meet the clients' needs. If you're shopping for a client who enjoys preparing gourmet meals on the weekends, you'll need to know what all those strange ingredients are and where you can locate them. If a client requests olive oil, do they want virgin or extra-virgin? When shopping for a new electronic device for a customer, what products and brands meet the client's needs and offer the best reliability, warranty, or service policy? Unless you are able to focus on a particular type of shopping, you'll probably need to familiarize yourself with a number of different items as well as the retail locations where you can purchase those items. But for someone who loves to shop, it's just part of the job.

Personal shopping isn't the career for everyone, especially if you don't enjoy shopping. But if you do, and you enjoy working for someone else, putting together a fabulous outfit, selecting just the right gift for a special occasion, or even just picking up the groceries, personal shopping might be a perfect fit for you.

Pitfalls

Personal shoppers may have difficulty making a full-time living in rural or small suburban areas. You may need to consider relocating if you hope to make a living as a personal shopper. From time to time you will have to deal with hard-to-please or difficult customers. And you may also face short deadlines if a client forgets that she needs an outfit or gift for an upcoming event.

Perks

Personal shoppers get to do something that they love while providing a valuable service to others. In some cases, they can specialize, and focus on buying certain items in which they are interested. Personal shopping can be a part-time job for someone who doesn't want to work full time, a student, or someone interested in pursuing other interests or business possibilities as well.

Get a Jump on the Job

Get a part-time job in retail services. Consider taking some classes in fashion, business, advertising, and marketing in high school or at a local junior or community college. If possible, job-shadow a personal shopper for several days or longer, or look for a summer job working for a shopper.

PIANO TECHNICIAN

OVERVIEW

With more than 12,000 parts, it's inevitable that at some time a piano will need some minor repair, or at the very least a tuning. In fact, for best sound and performance, a piano in a home that is played for fun and enjoyment should be tuned at least twice a year. Concert hall pianos are tuned before each use, which can mean once or twice a day.

To tune a piano, the technician loosens and tightens the strings so that they produce the correct tone (or pitch). But in some cases—especially with older pianos or with those that have not been cared for properly—the technician needs to do more than a simple tuning. In these cases, a good diagnosis is critical; with all those parts, the technician may need to be a detective of sorts to figure out exactly what's wrong and how to fix it.

Some people specialize in the restoration of older pianos, which can be complicated and painstaking work. Becoming a restorer requires additional training beyond that of a piano technician. With proper restoration and maintenance, a piano can survive 100 years or more.

Most piano technicians are self-employed, running small repair shops out of their home or a storefront. Because customers can't bring the piano into the shop for repair, the technician usually travels to the piano. As a result, a technician logs a lot of hours in the car. Other piano technicians work for music stores, piano manufacturers, school systems, college or university music departments, or in a performance

Brian Guikema-Bode, piano technician

For some, the career path is a clear, straight shot from beginning to end. For others, it is a road full of twists and turns, with the end a long way from the original starting point. That was the road Brian Guikema-Bode traveled. "I was going to be an English professor, so I went to college and earned a bachelor's degree and a master's degree and started teaching at Michigan State University," he says. But he quickly found out that the career he'd spent years preparing for wasn't a good fit for him. "I just didn't enjoy it," he explains. Next, he tried writing and editing, and discovered he wasn't fond of working in a windowless cubicle.

And then it all changed. "I made friends with a man who happened to be a piano tuner/ technician, and I was attracted to the lifestyle, especially being my own boss," he says. "You approach something not quite right and 'edit' it and make it right. I had an ear for it, so I entered into a two-year apprenticeship [with the man he had befriended]." One of the benefits of the apprenticeship, at least for Guikema-Bode, was that it was a good way to tell right away if you like the job or not.

It's not surprising that he was attracted to music, since both his parents were pianists and music was a huge part of his childhood. While not an accomplished pianist, Guikema-Bode himself does play the piano, as well as the trumpet and guitar—but playing the piano is not a requirement for piano tuning. "My master couldn't play the piano," he says. "He had memorized a little flourish that he would play. You don't have to have perfect pitch to do this, but good relative pitch. That is, if you hear a tone, you can duplicate it."

There are different reasons for people to become piano technicians, but one of the factors that influenced his decision was that he thinks pianos are amazing machines and engineering marvels, and he appreciates their beauty.

For someone with that appreciation for the instrument, there are many different areas in which to specialize. Some technicians rebuild old pianos, taking something that no longer works and restoring it to its original beauty and grandeur. Others only work on refinishing cases. Still others work for piano stores, working on instruments the store plans to sell; when pianos arrive from the manufacturer, they usually need some fine tuning or minor repairs. Finally, many technicians service pianos for private owners.

Guikema-Bode specializes in performance preparation, tuning for the Grand Rapids Michigan Symphony and other high-level artists. "[The pianist's] job is to inspire people and make the audience glad they paid money for the performance. My job is to make [the artist] happy."

It's a life he's learned to love. "I like being my own boss and setting my own schedule, I enjoy the experience of meeting people and being in lots of different situations." He also likes the fact that most of his jobs are short term, so that each new day brings new jobs with new problems and challenges. He's hard pressed to list things he doesn't like. Like most self-employed individuals, providing his own benefits is one of the biggest negatives, as is cash flow. The work is also physically demanding. "You see a lot of back problems in older technicians," he says. "Over time, [the work] can take its toll."

If you're interested in becoming a piano technician, he recommends that you go to a local piano shop or local guild and talk to piano techs. If you're interested in an apprenticeship, "make sure you find a master you can work with. Then hang out with the master for a month or so to make sure it's something you want to do."

And even though your ability to tune pianos is what will bring in work, it's also important to keep your customers happy with good people skills. "Some technicians have trouble because they look at it as a technical job," he says. "You fix what's wrong. But you have to deal with the person. Remember that as good as you are, the piano isn't writing the check, so keep your focus on your customer service."

setting such as a concert hall. Those piano technicians might also do tunings for individuals on the side in their free time.

There are several different ways to get the training you need to become a piano technician. You might enroll in a part- or full-time academic program, or take correspondence courses. Some also work as an apprentice for an established piano technician. Training programs generally last six months to two years, but it takes an additional two to five years of training and practice to become proficient at piano tuning and repair.

No matter where you study, there is a basic set of information that you need to learn. This basic core curriculum includes terminology, piano history, piano parts and how they work, tuning theory and procedures, common repairs, action and tone regulation, piano design, and basic business practices. If you hope to work for a college or university music department or in a performance setting, you may need college level training in piano technology. A list of training programs is available from the Piano Technician Guild (PTG).

The PTG offers its members the opportunity to earn the title of Registered Piano Technician (RPT) by passing a series of exams, including a written exam testing basic knowledge of piano design, tuning theory, repair, and general piano technology. A candidate must pass the written section with a score of at least 80 percent before trying the technical exam and tuning exam. Both the technical and tuning exams are about four hours and must be passed with a score of at least 80 percent.

Even after formal training, years of on-the-job experience, and RPT certification, piano technicians must still continue to keep up with the latest advances in piano technology. Published monthly, *The Piano Technicians Journal* contains a wealth of the latest up-to-date information for piano technicians. Technicians also stay up-to-date by participating in local PTG chapter events and attending the annual PTG convention.

Pitfalls

Piano repair can be very dirty, physical work. Since piano technicians usually work alone, there is little opportunity to interact with others who share similar professional interests. Depending on their geographic location, self-employed piano technicians may have to do a lot of travel to service enough customers to make a living, Also, self-employed piano technicians need to provide insurance and benefits for themselves and any employees they might have.

Perks

Many piano technicians are self-employed, giving them the freedom to set their schedule however they choose. Piano repair technicians also work under low stress conditions.

Get a Jump on the Job

Look for opportunities to work in a piano repair shop during summer vacations from school. Students very serious about becoming a piano technician might consider working on a correspondence course while still in high school to learn some of the basics before pursuing additional education and training after high school.

PROFESSIONAL ORGANIZER

OVERVIEW

How much time do you spend looking for your car keys, your cell phone, your gold drop earrings, your running shoes, or that book you promised you'd lend your best friend? According to *Newsweek*, a Boston marketing firm discovered that the average American spends 55 minutes a day looking for those things they know they own but just can't seem to locate. Think that sounds amazing? The National Association of Professional Organizers (NAPO) has a 27-page document with statistics detailing how much "stuff" people have, how much time and productivity people lose because of that stuff, and how much people truly want to get their lives organized. People spend billions of dollars a year on organizing products, but even with all those nifty organizing supplies, people aren't getting organized.

People like their stuff and they keep it for all sorts of reasons. They might keep the cracked tea cup because it belonged to a favorite great-aunt who used it every day for her afternoon tea. They hang on to that sweater they started knitting 20 years ago because one day they'll get around to finishing it. They keep the electric chicken roaster that's never been used because they paid good money for it, and who knows, maybe one day they'll need it. With all the personal attachments people have to their belongings, it's hard to just get rid of things. So sometimes when it's time to clean out and clean up, they call in the big guns: a professional organizer.

Professional organizers will help you organize nearly any room, situation, or problem aspect at home or at the office. For the residential client, an organizer might design, install, and organize closets. In the kitchen, they may rearrange and organize so that cooking is more efficient and items don't get lost in the back of the pantry. A client may ask the organizer to help with traditional storage areas such as the attic, basement, or garage, maybe even making it possible to get the cars back into the garage. Organizers also often organize home office spaces.

But it's not just spaces that an organizer will tackle. They may help the client deal with an overabundance of photos and how to store them properly. They might help a busy mom with her daily schedule so that things run better at home. Organizers will also come in and help clients organize an estate that they've inherited, help clients who are moving or relocating—they'll even organize garage and estate sales.

Debbie Stanley, professional organizer

You've seen those TV shows featuring organizational experts who trot into a client's house, act appalled at the degree of clutter, and then start throwing things away. In fact, a good professional organizer isn't some authoritarian "bad guy" telling clients what to do, but an adviser who can teach clients the necessary skills to change their behaviors and habits while projecting a nonjudgmental attitude.

"Disorganization is just a problem to be solved, not a character flaw!" explains professional organizer Debbie Stanley. Stanley admits that she was always the one organizing the supply cabinets and files when she worked in a traditional job environment. Her background includes a bachelor's degree in journalism and a master's degree in industrial/organizational psychology (which has to do with organizing groups of people, not spaces). One day, while poking around the Internet, Stanley came across the NAPO Web site. "I had heard of the phenomenon [of professional organizing] and found it was a perfect match for my skills and background," she says. Stanley had wanted to be self-employed anyway, so she decided to start her own organizing company.

For people who worry that being self-employed is a risky proposition, Stanley offers a unique perspective. "If I have a job in a regular company and my boss fires me, I'm unemployed. If I own my own business and have 30 clients at a time, that means all 30 people have to fire me all at once for me to be truly jobless."

She started slowly; it was three years before Stanley quit her "day" job to work full time as an organizer. Like many self-employed individuals, she doesn't care for the high costs to provide her own health insurance, the taxes, and the fact that things like getting a mortgage are more difficult. She says that she feels like small business owners are often treated like second class citizens, but the benefits outweigh the negatives.

Stanley says her clients get immediate gratification from her services; joking that the only other job where clients get the same immediate satisfaction is a chiropractor. "I go into a home or office, they tell me the problem, and I solve it." She says as a professional organizer you get to step into a life and make it better. "It's hugely rewarding, and I get to do it everyday."

Like most successful organizers, Stanley does more than just provide organizing services for clients. She warns, "You can't count on just billable hours. Too many client hours can burn you out. You need to find other ways to use your skills to bring in money." For Stanley those "other ways" include public speaking, writing, and teaching.

For a commercial client, the organizer typically focuses on making the workplace more ergonomic, arranging things so that the office runs more efficiently. If inventory control is a problem, the organizer may rearrange the warehouse space. An organizer can help employees who deal with large amounts of electronic information or e-mail, as well as paper documents. Organizers are also sometimes hired to help with time management issues and even to speak at employee meetings to address problem areas within the company.

Some organizers focus on services for specific client groups. They might provide services for children, students, senior citizens, or individuals with attention deficit disorder. In a corporate setting, organizers might specialize in services for legal offices, medical offices, manufacturing facilities, or

For someone interested in entering the field, Stanley says the industry is still growing. "It hasn't reached the tipping point yet. People are finding more and more ways to apply organizing skills to different situations." Stanley does think that we'll see more organizing firms hiring people on as professional organizers, so professional organizers won't have to be completely self-employed, like they are now.

When Stanley began in 1997 there was very little information on how to get started and nothing on how to organize, but that's all changing. Classes are available from NAPO, and they are in the process of developing a certification program that will help to legitimize the profession. Stanley drew on her own experiences to write *Newbie Pitfalls: 50 Obstacles on the Road to Success as Professional Organizer and How to Avoid Them!* She also offers a free monthly newsletter full of advice for both new and established professional organizers.

Basically, she believes there are three things someone needs to be a professional organizer: You need to be good at organizing, you need to be good at teaching, and you need to know how to run a business. "The most successful people draw on their personal experiences and backgrounds," she says. With all the different areas of specialization in the field of organizing, there's a fit for almost anyone. Stanley suggests doing a lot of research and self-evaluation to determine that "best fit."

If you want to pursue professional organizing, "Get involved with NAPO as quickly as you can afford to," she says. (Membership is $200 a year.) "You'll learn a lot of short cuts. It's a lot harder to go it alone. Why make mistakes you don't need to make?" She also recommends getting involved with a local NAPO chapter if possible, saying that overall, NAPO members are generous in sharing information with one another. They aren't generally threatened by one another because there are always more clients than organizers.

In addition, it's a good idea to attend the NAPO conference if at all possible, even if you aren't a member. Not only do the conferences have lots and lots of classes, but you also have an opportunity to meet your peers.

Stanley warns that you should be careful about throwing a lot of money at your business in the beginning, suggesting you set up a Web site first. "It's inexpensive and the best way to get up and running," she believes. Her Web site (http://www.rldpo.com) features a wealth of information, including details about the services she offers, answers to frequently asked questions, and a list of resources. You can also sign up for her newsletter while you are there.

employees with attention deficit disorder or other special needs.

Most organizers offer a variety of different organizing services; some services, such as feng shui, may require some specialized training.

When it comes to specific pieces of paper, that's usually up to the client; an organizer won't come in and start cleaning out a file cabinet. Instead, the organizer may discuss the situation and work with the clients to empower them to make the decisions about what needs to be kept and what can be discarded.

If you're interested in becoming a professional organizer and helping others get organized, NAPO offers a series of teleclasses about working as a professional organizer. To help both new and experienced organizers get more education, NAPO holds an annual conference.

Pitfalls

Most organizers are self-employed, so like most small business owners, lots of time needs to be spent building the business, which may not leave much time for actually helping clients get organized. Once established, an organizer will probably spend about half the time on marketing and bookkeeping. Organizers may have difficulty making a full-time living in rural or small suburban areas.

Perks

While organizing a client's home, office, or business, the organizer is really helping the client to organize his or her life. Once they're organized, clients usually find that they are more productive, happier, and less stressed. Organizing can be a part-time job, allowing someone to pursue other interests or business possibilities while also working as an organizer.

Get a Jump on the Job

Consider taking classes in business, advertising, accounting, marketing, and interior design in high school or at a local junior or community college. Read books on organizing (there are lots of them out there) to see what the pros are doing and to get ideas that you might be able to incorporate into your own organizing. Try to arrange an opportunity to shadow an organizer for several days. If possible, look for a summer or part-time job working for an organizer. You can even offer to organize for your family and friends to get some actual hands-on practice.

WATCH AND CLOCK REPAIRER

OVERVIEW

Most of the time, when a watch dies it's usually cheaper to replace it than to repair it. Advances in time-keeping technology—especially quartz and digital watches and clocks—have made them so affordable that most people own more than one watch and have a clock in each room of the house.

But that wasn't always the case. At one time, owning a watch or clock was a luxury. They were heirloom-quality pieces, with mechanical workings crafted to last a lifetime. Some expensive timepieces are still made with those types of mechanical parts, and it's those watches and clocks that repairers fix. The art of making and fixing watches and clocks is called *horology*; watch and clock repairers are sometimes called horologists.

When a watch or clock needs to be repaired, the owner will take the timepiece to an horologist at a jewelry shop or to a shop that specializes in watch or clock repair. The repairer will disassemble the timepiece and determine what needs to be fixed. Before getting to work, an estimate is usually given to the owner who decides if it's worth repairing the piece.

The timepiece may simply need a cleaning, adjustment, or winding, but quite often (especially with older timepieces), it will require a more extensive repair. Sometimes parts are completely worn out, and since replacement parts for older timepieces are not usually available, repairers will need to use

AT A GLANCE

Salary Range

The median hourly earning for individuals working as watch repairers is $12.77 per hour. The median annual earning for a highly skilled watch or clock repairer is more than $40,000 per year.

Education/Experience

Employers may prefer to hire individuals with at least a high school diploma or GED. Most watch and clock repairers learn their trade in formal training programs, occasionally they may have the opportunity to learn on the job. Many watch and clock repairers eventually open their own businesses, so classes in management, accounting, marketing, and other business-related topics would be very helpful.

Personal Attributes

Watch and clock repairers should be patient, detail-oriented, and accurate in their work. They need good problem-solving skills as well as a good understanding of how things work and how parts interact, along with the ability to read and comprehend technical materials and repair manuals. Good vision, manual dexterity, and finger strength is vital. Watch and clock repairers need to be self-starters and able to work well independently. They also need good social skills for dealing with customers.

Requirements

Self-employed watch or clock repair technicians will probably need to file Doing Business As (DBA) papers, secure a tax license, and acquire any other permits required under local and/or state ordinances.

Outlook

The number of jobs for watch and clock repairers is expected to increase more slowly than average. However, the average age of the 5,000 watch and clock repairers working today is 65. With few people entering the field to replace the aging workforce, there should be job opportunities for individuals interested in working as a watch or clock repairer.

small tools to machine the necessary part. Before reassembling the timepiece, it will be thoroughly cleaned and lubricated. The outside of the piece is usually cleaned and polished before it is returned to the owner.

Although watch and clock repairers spend most of their time in their shop repairing items, a clock repairer may occasionally venture out to diagnose and repair items that are too large for the customer to bring to the shop, such as a grandmother or grandfather clock. The repairer may take some pieces back to the shop for repairs, but in these cases, the bulk of the large-item work will be done on site.

You'll need extensive training to be able to repair watches or clocks. If you think that repairing fine and antique watches or clocks is the thing for you, there are several programs where you can learn the necessary skills. These programs can take from a few months to several years to complete; and can cost several thousand dollars. At least one home study course in clock repair is available.

Watch and clock repairs are studied in separate programs, and most clock repairers don't work on watches, and vice versa. While there are some similarities between the two timepieces and how they are repaired, there are many more differences than similarities between them. A repairer needs to learn the different skills and techniques required to repair each properly.

Clock programs generally take less time to complete than watch repair programs, because watch parts are smaller and require greater precision. Some parts may need to be machined or adjusted to within a fraction of a millimeter of design specifications for the watch to operate. Several professional associations offer various levels of certification. Watch and clock repairers learn new skills through continuing education classes, regional and national conventions, and symposiums sponsored by the major horological societies and associations.

Some students are able to study one-on-one or in small groups with a master repairer. Occasionally, a student is able to work as an apprentice to a watch or clock repairer, but apprenticeships aren't as common as they once were in the trade. This is because having an apprentice actually slows the repairer down, since he has to explain everything that he's doing to the student—and, by training an apprentice, the repairer is often training the person who will become his competition.

Regardless of how you gain the education, you can expect to learn a lot of new things. You will learn repair basics; disassembling, cleaning, oiling, reassembly, as well as basic theory and vocabulary. Some watches and clocks have problems and repairs that are specific to the particular type or brand of timepiece; you'll learn how to maintain and repair those watches and clocks. Much of your training will teach you how to use a variety of tools to create a part to fix a timepiece, when replacement parts are no longer available. You'll learn how to operate lathes, drill presses, mills, turns, grinders, polishers and other machine tools in the fabrication of repair parts. Some programs might also cover basic business practices, very important if you plan to open a shop of your own someday.

Most entry-level watch and clock repairers will begin their careers working for a more skilled repairer. This is an excellent way to continue learning and honing one's skills. Some watch repairers are employed by jewelry shops, repairing items for customers. Approximately 20 percent of watch and clock repairers are self-employed.

Robin Nance, certified clockmaker

During their formative years, children develop passions for all sorts of things, and those fascinations often develop into a lifelong ambition. The child fascinated with the planets may announce plans to become an astronaut, or the child in love with horses might dream of owning a stable. More often than not those childhood goals change over and over again as the child learns new things, meets new people, and has new experiences. That wasn't the case, however, for Robin Nance, who found his passion at the age of 14.

On a visit to his grandmother's house, he noticed a clock with no cord. "I asked how it worked, and I was just captivated by the fact that it worked by winding it." Already interested in mechanical things, Nance says, "I started buying old clocks [at garage sales and such] and reading how to repair them. My dad, who was an engineer at General Motors, introduced me to a fellow engineer who taught me the proper way to repair clocks." The two worked together repairing clocks throughout Nance's teens, as time allowed.

Although he continued to enjoy clocks as a hobby, as he grew older he began racing cars, eventually becoming a race car driver, driving open-wheel formula cars. He went on to teach at the world-famous Skip Barber Racing School. Yet as strange as it may sound, Nance says clock repair and racing actually have a lot in common. "The physics, science, mechanics, and [knowledge of] metals is the same as racing," he says. "You have to control the dynamics and be as accurate as possible."

As Nance got older he started to phase out the racing and decided to turn his hobby into his business. "I sold items from my own collection to buy more. And I started to do high-end antique shows selling restored clocks." Like racing, doing the antique circuit involved a lot of travel. "I was on the road 35 weeks a year. The rest of the time I was at home preparing clocks [to sell]." Nance eventually decided to settle down, repairing and selling clocks from his home in Dallas. Today, Nance and his wife Leslie run a clock repair and antique store.

Nance admits that clock repair is a dirty, low-paying job, and that it's necessary to work a lot of hours to make a living, but he loves what he does. "For me, making something work again is the most rewarding thing. I make a lot of people happy; I restore a lot of family pieces." He also enjoys being on his own, and having the freedom to choose his own workdays, as well as being able to travel to purchase clocks and other antiques for the shop.

Nance also enjoys teaching his customers about their clocks. "It's rewarding to see their interest grow," he says. "I teach them how to maintain their clock and use it properly. I want them to walk away with knowledge, because the more they know, the more they will treat it with respect."

If you're thinking of entering the trade, Nance recommends learning the proper way to do things. Clock repair is something that you should grow into, he says. "It can't be totally taught, but you need to have some professional beginnings. There are a lot of repair people who don't have the knowledge; I repair lots of other peoples' 'repairs.'"

Nance thinks there will be a need for qualified repair people in the future, especially for watch repairers, because where people may only own one clock, they will own several watches. For someone seriously considering entering this trade, he recommends reading some books on the subject and then spending some time talking to someone who does it for a living to get a good idea of what they do. Nance says he is always willing and happy to talk to someone interested in becoming a clock repairer.

To learn more about the services Nance offers, answers to some frequently asked questions, and view the clocks and other antiques Nance has uncovered on his journeys, you can visit his Web site at http://www.rclocks.com.

Pitfalls

Watch and clock repair is very solitary work; repairers often work alone, with little interaction with other repairers or customers. Self-employed repairers need to provide benefits for themselves and anyone they employ. Someone hoping to open a repair shop in a rural area may need to consider relocating to a more populated area to do enough business to pay the bills.

Perks

Self-employed watch and clock repairers can set their own hours; they can schedule days off and vacations when they want. Repairers keep memories alive repairing family heirlooms, and they get the opportunity to restore and repair a variety of antique timepieces. Many horologists truly love timepieces and find it relaxing to work on them.

Get a Jump on the Job

While in high school take as many practical, trade-related classes as possible. It's unlikely that you'll be able to take any watch or clock repair classes at your high school or vocational/technical center, but you can take drafting, machining, metalworking, mechanics, and introduction to business classes. Learning to read and understand technical manuals and drawings in also very important. If possible, look for a job working in a watch or clock repair shop during school vacations.

WEDDING PLANNER

OVERVIEW

As weddings these days become less about intimate personal experience and more Las Vegas-style extravaganza, the services of a wedding planner are in increasing demand. A wedding planner does just what the name suggests—he or she is involved in planning a wedding down to the tiniest detail, from selecting the wedding date to choosing the menu for the reception.

It may seem like one big lark, filled with yummy treats and vats of champagne, lots of pretty dresses and great music, but it takes months of planning to pull off a seemingly effortless wedding event. In fact, planning the perfect wedding day requires not only creativity and a sense of style, but also excellent business and organizational skills. (If it were easy, brides wouldn't need you to do it for them.)

Before you get to that moment when the bride begins her walk down the aisle, you must spend many hours planning, preparing and coordinating each and every detail, negotiating with a host of wedding vendors, dealing with clients and their families (who may be contentious)—as well as gracefully handling every bump in the road along the way.

Many wedding planners begin by working as a wedding coordinator at a hotel, country club, or resort in Hawaii, Las Vegas, Europe, or the Caribbean. Check out other job opportunities for bridal consultants with companies that provide products or services for weddings, such as bridal dress shops, large department stores, florists, and caterers. Once you have some

AT A GLANCE

Salary Range
$25,000 to $60,000 and up.

Education/Experience
Any college courses in marketing, business management, hospitality, or food and beverage areas is helpful. Specific training in wedding planning is provided by wedding consultant associations. Most consultants don't go to college to be a wedding planner; and most clients won't care about college experience. What matters here is wedding experience and creative flair. Certification as a wedding planner is offered through some wedding consultant organizations (see Appendix A).

Personal Attributes
Wedding planners should be creative people with excellent interpersonal skills who love to plan events, because they need to be able to juggle a myriad of responsibilities and remain calm in the midst of hysteria. It also helps to have excellent people skills with great communication, organizational, and negotiation ability.

Requirements
Although there are no national licensing requirements, some local jurisdictions do require licenses.

Outlook
Fair. While wedding planners are becoming more popular, they are still a luxury item, a "preference" service, not a necessity for the average couple planning a wedding.

experience in the business, you'll be ready to break out on your own.

No matter what your formal education, what really counts with clients is what you know about the wedding business. Couples will rely on you to understand and get them through the intricacies of the wedding industry. In order to be a

Sara L. Ambarian, wedding planner

Those beautifully-planned weddings with acres of ribbons, flowing gowns, and gorgeous centerpieces don't just happen—they're carefully crafted by a wedding planner just like Sara Ambarian.

Like most wedding planners, Ambarian didn't go to school to major in wedding planning—she spent years in the business learning the ropes. She graduated with honors from The Fashion Institute of Design and Merchandising with a degree in fashion design, and worked for more than 15 years in custom bridal gown and accessory design, and silk flower arranging. Before that, she'd worked in retail bridal, craft, fabric, and silk floral sales, tuxedo and bridal gown rentals, and alterations. By the time she was ready to launch her own wedding planning business, Ambarian knew the business inside and out.

"Actually, I am a wedding gown and accessory designer," she says. "Custom gowns, headpieces/veils, garters, shoe decoration, and silk bouquets and cake decorations have been my specialty since 1985, and they're my first and dearest professional love."

After working in the wedding industry for about eight years, she got the idea and the opportunity to write *A Bride's Touch: A Handbook of Wedding Personality and Inspiration*. "As a custom designer, I was working very intimately with my brides, and I realized that I wasn't just designing their attire and/or flowers. I was helping to 'design' their entire weddings. I was helping them with color coordination, etiquette questions, music and food ideas, diplomatic problems. So I just sort of added in the time for that to my fees for brides who wanted more help, and they were always happy to have one person they could really trust advising and supporting them."

In the mid-1990s, Ambarian says, everybody seemed to have the idea that weddings were stressful. You'd hear that idea everywhere, she says, from talk shows to wedding magazines to the evening news. "It was frustrating to me, because I knew from experience that weddings did not have to be stressful and something to be survived. It seemed like a horrible shame that that was pretty much the only message couples and their families were getting from media sources." By writing *A Bride's Touch,* Ambarian hoped to popularize a more realistic and practical message to more couples than she would have the opportunity to work with in a custom-design situation.

Once her book was published, she developed her own Web site and participated in some online wedding forums. "I was approached by a few sites to provide 'expert' answers and other information, and I started receiving e-mails and other contacts from brides and grooms and family members." The more specific creative wedding consulting services she offers separately from her design work mostly grew out of that Internet exposure and interest.

Many older wedding consultants/planners never trained specifically for consulting, she notes, and many didn't even think about consulting. "I never did, certainly," she says. "When I was growing up in the 70s and early 80s, bridal consultants were not nearly as popular as they were in the 90s or seem to be now. Mostly they seemed to be used by wealthy or famous brides for very large and elaborate ceremonies." Although a few girls of her generation decided they wanted to grow up and be a bridal consultant, it was clearly not a well-known career goal.

"That's why a career path to recommend to young women is hard to chart," she says. "The kinds of courses and accreditations being offered now didn't exist before, and while some seem to be useful, many may well just be opportunistic endeavors that leave both the graduate and their clients with a potentially false sense of security."

"I love all the creative parts: the beauty, the flowers and fabrics, the romance, the challenges—both in design and in diplomacy—the relationship I develop with my clients, the opportunity to be part of making a wonderful memory for a couple and their families." Less rewarding, she says, are some of the business issues, such as marketing and getting paid. "But I think that's common for anyone artistic working in a small business. If creative people could only afford to do what many doctors and dentists do now—hire an office manager to deal with issues of prices and payments, and just concentrate on the level of service they want to provide—it would be lovely. For most creative business people, we just have to bite the bullet and muddle through that stuff the best we can, because for most of us, it's the only way to get the opportunity to keep doing what we love to do."

Ambarian says she has mixed feelings about courses and associations. "I've not yet met anyone who's completed one of the courses and is working in the industry," she says. "I accessed part of a course outline for one of the wedding planner schools a few years ago, and I wasn't too enthused by it. It seemed to me that some real-world job experience in an actual wedding business or two, coupled with some good sense and the type of personal study I mention on my Web site, would actually give you as good an education than what they seemed to be teaching in that particular course." Ambarian also believes a positive attitude and a willingness to work hard to figure out anything you don't already know goes a long way toward being successful in this sort of business.

"I've found that every wedding is a little different, so each new client is a learning experience in some way," she says. "You need to have a good basic knowledge of weddings and related subjects, but you aren't ever going to be 'done' learning what you need to know to provide great advice to any given client. I sense that people taking courses expect that they'll be 'done' when they complete it and get their certificate. I'm not sure that's a good mindset."

She's also lukewarm about the value of professional associations. "I've read plenty of books and articles by people with great-looking credentials who say things I think are totally wrong or inappropriate to the way I personally view wedding issues. When people ask me on the Internet for advice about finding a good consultant or planner, I always stress that diplomas and memberships don't give you the whole package about a person's strengths and weaknesses. You need to talk to them about their philosophy, methods, past work, to get a feel for what they really know and how they really feel about working with you on something so personal."

Ambarian believes her best "instructors" have always been her clients. "They often don't know how to express what they need and want, but by getting them to trust and confide in me, I'm able to figure out how best to serve them."

She's had a number of couples with special issues, such as a tight budget, difficult family, stressful emergencies. "I'm always immensely proud when I see them overcome those issues, really enjoy themselves, and clearly have a wonderful wedding experience: brides who just shine with joy, pride, and confidence; grooms who shake my hand heartily and say the simplest 'thanks' with sincere emotion; a quick look of relief from a couple when I've diffused some family problem, or from a bride when I've intervened to get her an extra minute to herself before walking down the aisle. That's the kind of thing I remember.

"I've spent the last 20 years helping make the wedding fantasies of noncelebrities come true," she says. "I've worked with just about every style from simple and elegant traditionalism to breezy garden sweetness to savvy cocktail sophistication to Elizabethan pomp and opulence to upbeat swing retro to Old West cowboy charm. And every one of them was special to me, because every one of those weddings 'said' something about the couple it united. It was a very personal expression of their own personalities and unique relationship. For me, it's all about the couple."

really competent and professional planner, you need to have a really clear and complete understanding of the wedding industry and its products, services, policies and limitations.

Setting up a wedding planning business is pretty much like starting any other business. You can begin by working out of a home office, as long as you have a nice space where you can meet with clients. This way, you'll only have to pay for some office basics (such as a computer, fax, business phone, business cards, and so on). Once you've got your office set, you'll need to decide exactly what services to offer. Wedding planners are not all the same—some offer many more services than others. You'll need to decide what kind of services and packages to offer based on your specific skills and interests. For example, you might start out by offering only wedding day coordination, eventually expanding to offer complete wedding planning services. Some wedding planners specialize in arranging cruise ship weddings or "destination weddings" at resorts such as Walt Disney World. Decide which services you would like to offer.

You can't be a wedding planner without clients, so you'll need to focus on marketing your business and advertising. One of the best ways to find clients is by connections with wedding vendors, so leave your business card or brochure with bridal shops, caterers, florists, photographers, musicians, wedding DJs, and so on. Ask them to recommend your services to their customers. You'll also need to consider advertising in newspapers or magazines, participating in bridal shows, or even organizing your own bridal show. Because bridal magazines are so expensive, more and more wedding planners are advertising on the Internet. Because modern brides

typically know their way around the Internet, they surf the Web to research vendor choices and options. You'll need to budget at least $1,000 for a professional Web site design to give the most professional impression you can.

As part of your marketing plan, you should put together a portfolio—a collection of photographs that show people how you've done other weddings. To develop a portfolio like this, you can offer your services for free to friends and family who are getting married in exchange for portfolio photos; they can also supply you with reference letters. In the portfolio, include photographs of table settings or room decorations you've created at home, or pictures from your own wedding.

When you get a call from a prospective bride, you'll need to arrange a client consultation meeting to learn as much as you can about the couple and what they want. Once you find out their interests, you can show them how you can help them achieve the wedding of their dreams. You'll need to find out what type of wedding they want, what their budget is, how many guests there will be, and so on. At this meeting you'll also discuss your fees, which might range from an hourly fee to a flat salary. You'll need to help brides select or design their bridal gowns and accessories, choose wedding colors and mood, select or arrange flowers, select appropriate music for different parts of the wedding, and select the invitations, decorations, and refreshments. Then you'll need to decide on the timing and schedule for the ceremony and reception. All throughout the process, you'll need to help calm the bridal stress and provide help with etiquette questions.

As these decisions are being made, to help you stay organized, you should create timeline schedules and checklists, and use organizational tools such as a day planner or binder to keep track of all the wedding details.

To be successful, you should have a true love of weddings, fine fabrics, color and style, and enjoy the challenge of making each wedding unique. It helps to have a good background of interest, knowledge, and experience in a wide range of subjects, such as historical and theatrical costumes, literature, traditions, crafts, sewing, art, cooking, botany/horticulture, and travel. It's also helpful to have an ability to envision settings that don't yet exist, and a natural eye for color, texture, harmony, and style. Most important is a deep intuitive instinct for seeing and understanding the needs and desires of brides, when even they sometimes aren't sure what they want.

Pitfalls

You can expect to encounter a fair amount of startup money, since you'll need to advertise your business, which can be a very big investment. Some bridal magazines ad can cost thousands of dollars. You'll also need business liability insurance and a professionally-designed Web site. Consider joining a professional association for wedding planners to keep up with new developments in the industry. Like all self-employed individuals, you'll need to pay your own expenses, you won't have any paid vacation, and if you don't work, you don't earn. You may work very long hours at certain times, depending on the work load and the season—especially if you have more than one client. Be prepared to work evenings and weekends, as well as weekdays, and you should expect to work a lot of Friday night rehearsals and all-day Saturday weddings.

Perks

Wedding planners are typically outgoing, creative types who love to organize and plan, so what could be more fun than planning a wedding, a person's most joyous personal event? Most people are happy and in a good mood at this time, and you'll be surrounded by lots of joy.

Get a Jump on the Job

If you're the born organizing type and you think you'd enjoy working as a wedding planner, you can start by reading up on weddings and attending or helping out with as many weddings as possible. You can visit bridal shows, read wedding magazines, and conduct interviews with clergy of various faiths, recently married brides, wedding photographers or entertainers, and anyone else connected to the wedding business, such as florists and caterers.

APPENDIX A. ASSOCIATIONS, ORGANIZATIONS, AND WEB SITES

AAA HOTEL RATER

American Automobile Association
1000 AAA Drive
Heathrow, FL 32746
http://www.aaa.com

As North America's largest motoring and leisure travel organization, AAA provides its members with travel, insurance, financial, and automotive-related services. Since its founding in 1902, the nonprofit AAA has been a leader and advocate for the safety and security of all travelers.

AAA TourBooks
http://www.aaanewsroom.net/Main/
Default.asp?CategoryID=9&SubCategor
yID=25&ContentID=94&
Web site explaining the details of the AAA TourGuide books.

AMERICAN SIGN LANGUAGE INTERPRETER

American Consortium of Certified Interpreters (ACCI)
7602 Murray Drive, Suite 106
Stockton, CA 95210
(209) 475-4837 (TTY/Voice)
http://www.acci-iap.org

The American Consortium of Certified Interpreters (ACCI) National Sign Language Interpreter Assessment Program is designed to evaluate and certify qualified candidates to serve as sign language interpreters. These individuals facilitate communication between deaf and hearing people in a variety of settings,
including employment and training, education, health care, community service, and social welfare environments.

Gallaudet University Graduate School and Professional Programs
800 Florida Avenue, NE
Washington, DC 20002
(800) 995-0513
PST@gallaudet.edu
http://gspp.gallaudet.edu

Gallaudet University offers nondegree credit ASL and Interpreter Education courses during summer intensive "immersion" courses. Program information can be obtained by contacting the above address.

Gallaudet University Department of Interpretation
800 Florida Avenuenue, NE
Washington, DC 20002
(202) 651-5450
http://interpretation.gallaudet.edu

Gallaudet offers a program leading to a Master of Arts degree in Interpreting. For information on this program, contact the address above.

Registry of Interpreters for the Deaf
333 Commerce Street
Alexandria, VA 22314
(703) 838-0030 (Voice)
(703) 838-0459 (TTY)
pr@rid.org
http://www.rid.org

The Registry of Interpreters for the Deaf, Inc. (RID) is a national membership organization of professionals who provide sign language interpreting/transliterating services for deaf and hard of hearing people. RID provides information on the national, state, or local chapters of the RID, the interpreter certification and certification maintenance process, a list of publications, and other matters relevant to the interpreting profession.

AQUARIUM MAINTENANCE SERVICE PROVIDER

AquaRank
http://www.aquarank.com

AquaRank is a listing of the top 250 aquarium Web sites based on votes from aquarium enthusiasts, hobbyists, and professionals around the world. The list is re-ranked every 10 minutes. A search engine makes it easy to find Web sites on a specific topic. With all the fish information on the Web, this site is very helpful for someone just getting into the fish field.

American Marinelife Dealers Association (AMDA)
Attn: Liz Harris
c/o Creatures Featured
PO Box 1052
Madison, FL 32341
(850) 973-3488
http://www.amdareef.com

Founded in 1995, the American Marinelife Dealers Association (AMDA) is a nonprofit organization "promoting sustainable trade in living marine organisms for aquariums." Members include retailers, importers, breeders, service providers, and hobbyists. The AMDA is working to establish a set of business standards (for marinelife dealers), and a network of businesses that adhere to those standards. They are also working to increase awareness and education in the areas of conservation, animal husbandry, responsible handling, and captive breeding. Archived newsletters are available online.

American Zoo and Aquarium Association (AZA)
8403 Colesville Road, Suite 710
Silver Spring, MD 20910-3314
(301) 562-0777
http://www.aza.org

The American Zoo and Aquarium Association (AZA) began as the American Association of Zoological Parks and Aquariums in 1924. The AZA is a nonprofit organization committed to the preservation and advancement of zoos and aquariums. For anyone considering earning an advanced (college) degree with the hope of eventually working for a zoo or aquarium, this is an excellent site with information about job listings, professional training, conferences and meetings, news, grants, and much, much more.

Marine Aquarium Council (MAC)
923 Nu'uanu Avenue
Honolulu, HI 96817
(808) 550-8217
info@aquariumcouncil.org
http://www.aquariumcouncil.org

The Marine Aquarium Council (MAC) is a nonprofit organization committed to the conservation of the coral reefs and other marine ecosystems. Members include hobbyists, retailers, importers, and exporters, as well as public aquariums, conservation groups, and government agencies worldwide. To make it easy to find the best and most pertinent information for each situation, the site has sections for the hobbyists (or keeper), individuals in the industry, public aquarium managers and employees, conservationists, and government agencies.

Marine Aquarium Societies of North America (MASNA)
http://www.masna.org

The Marine Aquarium Societies of North America (MASNA) is another nonprofit organization for hobbyists with an interest in marine aquariums. The organization works to educate members, encourage the marine tank hobby, and eliminate abusive practices in the collecting and transporting of marine life. The Web site is a wealth of information for marine enthusiasts. It has an extensive list of links on the subject as well as a chat room and forum (ReefTalk).

ReefCentral

http://www.reefcentral.com

ReefCentral is an online community of marine and reef tank enthusiasts. An excellent resource with discussion forums, a photo gallery, do-it-yourself projects, tank of the month, links, a chat room, and much, much more. Search tools make it easier to find what you are looking for. Registration is required (and free), but definitely worth it. If it's marine or reef related, you'll find it at ReefCentral.

BEER TAP CLEANER

Probrewer.com

http://www.probrewer.com

An online resource serving all trades of the specialty beer business. The Web site offers tools and materials to help anyone in the beer business, from the technical side of brewing to sales and distribution. ProBrewer.com is dedicated to empowering the specialty beer segment through the dissemination of comprehensive, current, and relevant information.

BIKE MESSENGER

International Federation of Bike Messenger Associations

PO Box 191443
San Francisco, CA 94119
http://www.messengers.org/ifbma

Nonprofit organization founded to foster a spirit of cooperation and community amongst bicycle messengers worldwide, and to promote the use of pedal power for commercial purposes.

The District of Columbia Bicycle Courier Association

http://www.dccourier.com/dcbca

The District of Columbia Bicycle Courier Association is a not-for-profit organization dedicated to protecting the rights of bicycle couriers in Washington, D.C.; helping to ensure the future of the bike courier industry by establishing an equitable understanding between couriers, the businesses they serve, and the communities they interact with; and promoting the bicycle as an alternative means of transportation.

The New York Bike Messenger Association

51 MacDougal Street, Suite 271
New York, NY 10012
(212) 726-1BMA
http://www.nybma.com/contacts.htm

The New York Bicycle Messenger Foundation was established in 2003 as a nonprofit corporation to provide aid and financial assistance to bicyclists and pedestrians who are injured on New York City streets. This aid may be in the form of either funding for health care and rehabilitation for the injured party or direct financial assistance to those in need of these funds while they recover from their injuries. Along with these primary purposes, the NYBMF also strives to unify the bicycle courier community to help achieve charitable goals. The Web site offers an online store, a bike messenger forum, and information about messenger events.

BODY PARTS MODEL

Parts Models
PO Box 7529 FDR Station
New York, NY 10150
(212) 744-6123
http://www.partsmodels.com/aboutus.html

Parts Models, based in New York City, is the leading model agency specializing in models for body parts. The agency was founded in 1986 to provide hand, leg, feet, and body models for editorial, advertising, and catalog work. Parts models are seen in the editorial pages of national publications such as Vogue, Glamour, Mademoiselle, Allure, Town & Country, McCall's, Men's Health, *and* Fitness.

BRAILLE TRANSCRIBER

The American Braille Career School
PO Box 3686
Salem, OR 97302
(877) 515-4095
http://www.brailleplus.net/school

The ABC School was founded to meet the need for Braille transcribers in the United States and throughout the world. The school is a division of Braille Plus, Inc., an internationally recognized provider of alternate formats for the visually impaired. Graduates of this school earn a Literary Braille Certification.

American Printing House for the Blind
1839 Frankfort Avenue
Louisville, KY 40206
(800) 223-1839
info@aph.org
http://www.aph.org

Associated Services for the Blind
919 Walnut Street
Philadelphia, PA 19107
(215) 627-0600

asbinfo@asb.org
http://www.asb.org

California Transcribers and Educators of the Visually Handicapped (CTEVH)
http://www.ctevh.org

Library of Congress, National Library Services for the Blind and Physically Handicapped
(800) 424-8567
http://www.loc.gov/nls/bds.html

This service offers a free correspondence course at all levels. They will fax or mail you an application.

National Braille Association
3 Townline Circle
Rochester, NY 14623-2513
(585) 427-8260
http://www.nationalbraille.org

The mission of the National Braille Association is to provide continuing education to those who prepare braille, and to provide braille materials to persons who are visually impaired.

National Braille Press
88 St. Stephen Street
Boston, MA 02115
(888) 965-8965
orders@nbp.org
http://www.nbp.org

BROADCAST CAPTIONER

National Court Reporters Association
8224 Old Courthouse Road
Vienna, VA 22182
(800) 272-6272
msic@ncrahg.org
http://www.ncraonline.org

NCRA is committed to advancing the profession of court reporting through ethical standards, testing and certification, educational programs, contacts with lawmakers, research and analysis. Almost all broadcast captioners begin by being court reporters, so this organization is helpful. NCRA members are offered certification exams in May and November. The association promotes a code of professional ethics. NCRA also offers information about online training for court reporters. It has a Virtual Mentors program that allows high school or college students to get in touch with court reporters. Through the National Court Reporters Foundation, the NCRA uses charitable support to promote research, technology, and education in court reporting. NCRA works on behalf of an international membership to influence legislation that will affect court reporters.

BUTLER

International Butler Academy
http://www.butlerschool.com

This unique and exclusive nonprofit butling and house management school promotes the butling and the private service profession by training dedicated individuals in becoming professionals in the art of butling and house management. The International Butler Academy provides its graduates with the best possible qualifications for entering the private service profession. The comprehensive eight-week, government-licensed course will introduce and test each student in all the expected duties of a butler/personal assistant/valet and house manager. Although a large part of your responsibility as a butler could be serving meals, setting tables, etc. and you will receive ample training in these areas, the overall training mainly focuses on how to professionally run and manage a large, multimillion dollar estate.

International Guild of Professional Butlers
134 West 82nd Street, Suite 3B
New York, NY 10024

(212) 877-6962
http://www.butlersguild.com

Members and contacts include butlers, personal assistants, private chefs, couples, estate managers, house managers, housekeepers, nannies, property managers, hotel butlers, private service consultants, and other domestic specialists. The guild also offers a free advisory service to employers of private staff and members of the public on any matter related to private service and the recruitment of private staff.

Charles MacPherson Associates
134 West 82nd Street, Suite 3B
New York, NY 10024
(212) 877-6962
http://www.charlesmacpherson.com/index.html

Founded in 1996, Charles MacPherson Associates is a residential management systems company dedicated to the development and implementation of custom solutions to help staff operate a property in a professional, efficient, and cost-effective manner. Charles MacPherson Associates' clients include individuals and families with single or multiple private residences. Operating from offices in Toronto and New York, Charles MacPherson Associates has successfully implemented residential management systems for a long list of clients in the United States, Canada, and Europe.

CAREER COUNSELOR

National Career Development Association (NCDA)
305 North Beech Circle
Broken Arrow, OK 74012
(866) FOR-NCDA [367-6232]
http://www.ncda.org

The NCDA is a division of the American Counseling Association. Founded in 1913 as the National Vocational Guidance Association, it was renamed the National Career Development Association in 1985. The primary mission of NCDA is to promote the career development of all people. The NCDA meets this goal by providing service individuals, both public and professional, working in or simply interested in career development. Membership benefits include subscriptions to both the NCDA journal and newsletter, online forums, an annual conference with continuing education programs, and networking opportunities with other NCDA members. The NCDA Web site is a terrific source of information for someone considering career counseling, but even if you're not interested in helping someone else find the perfect job, stop by to check out the 18 pages of Internet Sites for Career Planning to help you find your perfect job.

ETIQUETTE CONSULTANT

International Association of Protocol Consultants
PO Box 6150
McLean, VA 22106
(703) 759-4272

The IAPC provides executive education in leadership, international protocol, etiquette, and civility, and offers two certification programs for certified protocol consultant and certified protocol officer.

FITTING MODEL

Rage Modeling Agency
23501 Park Sorrento
Calabasas, CA 91302
(818) 225-0526
http://www.ragemodels.com

Modeling agency specializing in "real" models, including fitting models.

Shay Taylor
http://www.shaysworld.com
Website of fit model Shay Taylor, with lots of information about the job of fit model.

FORTUNE COOKIE WRITER

Weird Fortune Cookie Collection
http://www.weirdfortunecookies.com
This Web site collects weird fortunes sent in by alert readers.

Wonton Food, Inc.
220-222 Moore Street
Brooklyn, NY 11206
(800) 776-8889
http://www.wontonfood.com/company_profile.htm

The largest producer of fortune cookies in the United States, and sponsor of an annual fortune writing contest.

FUNERAL DIRECTOR

The American Board of Funeral Service Education
38 Florida Avenue
Portland, ME 04103
http://www.abfse.org/index.html

The American Board of Funeral Service Education (ABFSE) serves as the national academic accreditation agency for college and university programs in funeral service and mortuary science education. ABFSE is the sole accrediting agency recognized by the U.S. Department of Education and the Council on Higher Education Accreditation in this field.

Funeral Staff
4430 Wade Green Road, Suite 180-138
Kennesaw, GA 30144
(770) 966-8048
http://www.funeralstaff.com

FuneralStaff is a professional, full service staffing and consulting firm specializing in placing funeral service professionals, administrators, and support staff. With almost 20 years of combined experience in funeral service and executive staffing services, Funeral Staff can help funeral service candidates find opportunities with some of the finest funeral homes, crematories, cremation societies, pre-need or cemetery organizations in the country.

The National Funeral Directors Association
13625 Bishop's Drive
Brookfield, WI 53005
http://www.nfda.org

This association offers information about college programs in mortuary science, scholarships, and funeral service as a career.

FUNERAL HOME COSMETOLOGIST

The American Board of Funeral Service Education
38 Florida Avenue
Portland, ME 04103
http://www.abfse.org/index.html

The American Board of Funeral Service Education (ABFSE) serves as the national academic accreditation agency for college and university programs in funeral service and mortuary science education. ABFSE is the sole accrediting agency recognized by the U.S. Department of Education and the Council on Higher Education Accreditation in this field.

Funeral Staff
4430 Wade Green Road, Suite 180-138
Kennesaw, GA 30144
(770) 966-8048
http://www.funeralstaff.com

FuneralStaff is a professional, full service staffing and consulting firm specializing in placing funeral service professionals, administrators, and support staff. With almost 20 years of combined experience in funeral service and executive staffing services, Funeral Staff can help funeral service candidates find opportunities with some of the finest funeral homes, crematories, cremation societies, pre-need or cemetery organizations in the country.

National Accrediting Commission of Cosmetology Arts & Sciences
4401 Ford Avenue, Suite 1300
Alexandria, VA 22302
(703) 600-7600
http://www.naccas.org/index.html

The National Accrediting Commission of Cosmetology Arts and Sciences (NACCAS) is an independent accrediting commission founded in 1969, when two accrediting agencies in the field merged to form the Cosmetology Accrediting Commission (CAC). CAC changed its name to NACCAS in 1981. NACCAS is recognized by the US. Department of Education as a national agency for the institutional accreditation of postsecondary schools and departments of cosmetology arts and sciences, including specialized schools. It presently accredits about 1,000 institutions with more than 100,000 students, offering more than 20 courses and programs of study.

The National Funeral Directors Association
13625 Bishop's Drive
Brookfield, WI 53005
http://www.nfda.org

This association offers information about college programs in mortuary science, scholarships, and funeral service as a career.

GOVERNESS

English Nanny & Governess School, Inc.
37 South Franklin Street
Chagrin Falls, OH 44022
(800) 733-1984
http://www.nanny-governess.com

America's nanny school that also offers a governess certification program, and is dedicated to the education of professional nannies and governesses in the field of early childhood education.

HOLIDAY DECORATOR

American Holiday Decorators Association
36 Hillman Street, Unit 4
Tewksbury, MA 01876
(978) 858-0250
Member_Services@ahda.com
http://ahda.com

The American Holiday Decorators Association (AHDA) is a nonprofit organization for professional holiday decorators as well as suppliers of holiday lights and decorating items. The AHDA allows members to connect with one another; networking and sharing ideas and information. It also allows decorators and suppliers to connect with each other. As a professional organization for one of the fastest growing service industries, the AHDA strives to represent, educate, and promote the holiday decorating industry. Membership includes a newsletter published every three to four months. It also includes complete access to the association's Web site, which features a members' only message board, making it easy for members to connect and get quick answers to their questions and problems.

Christmas Décor
206 23rd Street
Lubbock, TX 79404
(806) 722-1225
http://www.christmasdecor.net

With more than 400 franchises nationwide, Christmas Décor is one of the largest Christmas decorating companies in the country. The Web site lets you find Christmas Décor decorators in your area, or determine that the market is still available. While you are there, check out the portfolio featuring just a fraction of the more than 32,000 projects Christmas Décor decorators have done. For someone seriously interested in investing in a Christmas Décor franchise, there is extensive information about the benefits that their franchisees enjoy, including training, support, and marketing.

Creative Decorating
7535 Graceland Drive
Omaha, NE 68134-4330
(888) 251- 8799
http://www.creativedecoratinginc.com

For individuals wanting to open a holiday decorating business but don't have the money or desire to buy a franchise, Creative Decorating's founder, Brad Finkle has put together a training manual and set of videotapes that take a beginner step-by-step through setting up and growing an exterior Christmas decorating business.

Holiday and Home Expo
Dallas Market Center
2100 Stemmons Freeway
Dallas, TX 75207
(214) 655-6100
http://www.dallasmarketcenter.com

Organized by Dallas Market Center, the Holiday & Home Expo features the new products and the latest trends in home and holiday decorating.

PlanetChristmas Corporation
245 Pebble Glen Drive

Franklin, TN 37064
(615) 301-1671
http://www.planetchristmas.com

PlanetChristmas is a Web site for holiday light enthusiasts. But with its vast wealth of information, it's an excellent resource for someone interested in the holiday decorating business. The site features a chatroom where you can post your holiday lighting questions and get answers. A question-and-answer section covers many topics. For a little inspiration, or holiday cheer in July, check out the more than 100 photos in the "Showing Off" section. There's also an extensive list of vendors, useful links, and much more.

Plantscape, Inc.
3101 Liberty Avenue
Pittsburgh, PA 15201
(412) 281-6352
http://www.plantscape.com

Each year, more than 60 of Plantscape's "elves" fan out across the Pittsburgh area and decorate more than 300 businesses. The Plantscape elves have won close to 30 national awards for their business Christmas Decorating. In the June of even years, the elves share their knowledge at training seminars attended by people from around the country. The biennial conferences feature a decorator's awards contest as well as an opportunity for decorators to network with other decorators. Plantscape also offers a complete line of holiday decorating items. If you happen to be in the Pittsburgh area, be sure to stop by and visit their 7,000 square-foot showroom.

HOME STAGER

Staged Homes
4807 Clayton Road, Suite 100
Concord, CA 94521

(800) 392-7161
http://www.stagedhomes.com

StagedHomes.com was founded by Barb Schwarz, the creator of home staging, and she serves as its CEO. The site offers excellent information about staging, including the history of staging and tips for home sellers and much, much more. You can learn about the ASP training courses, and when and where they are being held. The site features many before and after pictures. While you are there, you can read about staging in the news, listen live to Schwarz's weekly radio show, or check out the archive of previously aired shows. Every individual who completes the ASP program has a profile page at the StagedHomes site, so you can see what stagers are doing in your hometown, or across the country.

International Association of Home Staging Professionals (IAHSP)
4807 Clayton Road, Suite 200
Concord, CA 94521
(925) 686-2413
http://www.iahsp.com

Founded in 2000, the International Association of Home Staging Professionals (IAHSP) is the professional organization for Accredited Staging Professionals (ASPs). IAHSP brings home stagers together to network, brainstorm, and share information through conference calls, conventions, and regional chapters. A newsletter allows stagers to stay current on what's new in the world of staging with information about upcoming events, articles from fellow members, motivational ideas, as well as covering new ideas, products, and tools that really work. IAHSP members enjoy huge marketing benefits. On the third Saturday of each September, the IAHSP celebrates Community Worldwide

Staging Day. On this day, regional chapters give back to their community by providing their (staging) services to hospitals, food banks, shelters, crisis centers, and other community organizations.

HOTEL CONCIERGE

International Concierge and Errand Association
4932 Castor Avenue
Philadelphia, PA 19124
(800) 934-ICEA
http://iceaweb.org

The International Concierge and Errand Association (ICEA) is a nonprofit trade association founded in 2001 designed to meet the professional needs of Concierge and Errand business owners worldwide. ICEA offers members business support, networking opportunities, continuing education, advocacy, and industry recognition. ICEA is the leading global professional association committed to supporting the owners and operators of concierge and errand service businesses, serving as the primary resource and active advocate for our members through essential resources, continuing education, networking opportunities, and other professional endeavors.

Les Clefs d'Or USA
68 Laurie Avenue
Boston, MA 02132
http://lcdusa.org

The only national association of professional hotel concierges in the United States. It was founded to foster the professional development of hotel concierges by promoting tourism and the highest standards of service for

hotel guests, and has more than 450 members in more than 30 states.

National Concierge Association
(612) 317-2932
info@nationalconciergeassociation.com
http://www.nationalconciergeassociation.com

The National Concierge Association (NCA) grants membership status to concierge professionals and vendors alike.

Triangle Concierge
3650 Rogers Road, #328
Wake Forest, NC 27587
(919) 453-2850
info@triangleconcierge.com
http://www.triangleconcierge.com

The world's premier international concierge training and consulting company. We train both individuals and companies how to create their own concierge and/or Lifestyle Management Company. Since 1998, Triangle Concierge has provided cutting edge concierge products and services to thousands of clients from both small and large companies in the United States, across Canada and almost 30 countries around the world.

INNSITTER

Interim Innkeepers Association
http://www.interiminnkeepers.net/members/member_pages/TheSunriseInnsitter.html

A nonprofit association of innkeepers who are trained and experienced in providing relief innkeeping services to B&Bs, country inns, and boutique hotels. Members include short- and long-term innsitters.

LOCKSMITH

Associated Locksmiths of America
3500 Easy Street
Dallas, TX 75247
(800) 532-2562
http://www.aloa.org

The Associated Locksmiths of America (ALOA) is an international association of security professionals (which includes locksmiths). They offer continuing education as well as several levels of certifications. There are active ALOA chapters and affiliates throughout the United States and around the world. You can find the chapter nearest you at http://www.aloa.org/about/ChapsAndFils.php. A list of locksmithing schools is maintained on ALOA's Web site (http://www.aloa.org/pdf/locksmithingschools.pdf). The ALOA offers scholarships to the convention as well as for continuing education and other training to qualified individuals. The ALOA also sponsors a yearly convention.

Institutional Locksmiths' Association
PO Box 24772
Philadelphia, PA 19111
http://ilanational.org

The Institutional Locksmiths' Association (ILA) is a not-for-profit association of locksmiths and other individuals who provide locksmithing services to colleges and universities, hospitals, government facilities, and companies. The association was created to give those individuals a forum and network to discuss issues unique to locksmithing in an institutional setting. The ILA offers several levels of certification, and they hold an annual, national conference.

Locksmith Ledger International
3030 Salt Creek Lane, Suite 200
Arlington Heights, IL 60005
http://www.lledger.com

For nearly 60 years, locksmiths have been reading Locksmith Ledger International *(the* Ledger*), the magazine of the locksmith trade. Also known as the "Bible of the industry," today 12,500 subscribers turn to the pages of the* Ledger *each month to stay current on all the advances in locksmithing.*

MATCHMAKER

Matchmaking Institute: The School of Matchmaking & Relationship Sciences
89 Fifth Avenue, Suite 602
New York, NY 10003
(212) 242-0965
http://www.matchmakinginstitute.com

The Matchmaking Institute was founded in 2003 as a professional organization for matchmakers with the goal of setting standards and a code of ethics for the industry. To meet these goals, they have established an educational institute, and they supply the tools and materials individuals need to get started in a matchmaking career. So far, they have trained students from over 30 states as well as 4 foreign countries in their training program approved by the New York State Education Department. The program consists of 11 classes done over the course of a three-day weekend at the Institute's New York City headquarters. To help matchmakers grow in their profession, The Institute has established the Matchmakers NetworkSM as a forum for experienced matchmakers to exchange ideas, practical experiences, and knowledge. You can sign up to receive a newsletter specifically for individuals who want to become a matchmaker (they also have a newsletter for individuals looking for a matchmaker as well as one for people who are matchmakers.) The Web site features biographies of member matchmakers where you can learn a little bit more about the types of people making matches for a living and a little bit about their businesses.

MYSTERY SHOPPER

Mystery Shopping Providers Association (MSPA)
12300 Ford Road, Suite 135
Dallas, TX 75234
(972) 406-1104
http://www.mysteryshop.org

With more than 150 member companies around the world, the MSPA is the largest trade association for mystery shopping in the world. The MSPA offers two levels of Shopper Certification. The first level (Silver Certification) is available online; the second level (Gold Certification) is earned through an on-site workshop, which the MSPA offers at various locations around the country throughout the year. Potential shoppers can learn a lot about the profession through numerous newspaper and magazine articles archived at the MSPA Web site. Shoppers also can search for job assignments at the MSPA Web site. Members have an opportunity for networking and training at annual MSPA conferences. Those unable to attend the conferences can network with other shoppers through the MSPA forum (http:// www.mysteryshop.org/shoppers/forum).

National Center for Professional Mystery Shoppers & Merchandisers (NCPMS, Inc.)
PO Box 311573
Tampa, FL 33680
http://www.ncpmscenter.org

The NCPMS is a not-for-profit organization established to provide education and support to mystery shoppers and merchandisers. They provide education through their Professional Learning Center, offering several different certification programs. All of their programs are available completely online. Shoppers and merchandisers are able to communicate with one another and offer support to one another through a huge and extremely active forum area. Shoppers also can get information on potential jobs through a NCPMS-sponsored e-mail list where schedulers post job leads and news (http://finance.groups.yahoo. com/group/mysteryshoppingbyncpms). A FAQ section has great resources for not only new shoppers but established ones as well, including getting started, information about certification, handling payment issues, sample letters, a dictionary of industry terms, hot links, and more.

ShadowShopper
21175 Tomball Parkway, Suite 387
Houston, TX 77070
http://www.shadowshopper.com

ShadowShopper was voted the Mystery Shopping Referral Service of the Year by the National Center for Professional Mystery Shoppers & Merchandisers in both 2003 and again in 2004. Their site is a wealth of information for beginning mystery shoppers. The "Shopper University" section has dozens of informative articles covering all facets of mystery shopping. Some of the articles and other information are for members only. Various levels of memberships are available for a fee. Even without a membership, there are many resources you can access.

NANNY

4nannies.com

Lists hundreds of open nanny and household staffing jobs from across the

United States and beyond, including live-in or live-out, full time or part time, elder care or housekeeping jobs. Nannies can apply for jobs here using a free online registration form.

International Nanny Association
191 Clarksville Road
Princeton Junction, NJ 08550-3111
(888) 878-1477
http://www.nanny.org

Established in 1985, the INA is a nonprofit, educational association for nannies and those who educate, place, employ, and support professional in-home child care providers. Membership is open to those who are directly involved with the in-home child care profession including nannies, nanny employers, nanny placement agency owners (and staff), nanny educators, and providers of special services related to the nanny profession.

National Association of Nannies
25 Route 31 South, Suite C
Pennington, NJ 08534
(800) 344-6266
http://www.nannyassociation.com

The association strives to promote the nanny as an occupation and as a profession. The association Web site offers information about national conferences, awards, a newsletter, and support groups.

Nanny Network
Home/Work Solutions, Inc.
2 Pigeon Hill Drive, #550
Sterling, VA 20165
(703) 404-8964
http://www.nannynetwork.com/contact.cfm

The Traveling Nanny
(850) 321-3239
http://www.thetravelingnanny.com

PAGEANT CONSULTANT

Miss America
Two Miss America Way, Suite 1000
Atlantic City, NJ 08401
(609) 345-7571
info@MissAmerica.org
http://www.missamerica.org

Developed by the Miss America Organization, the Miss America program exists to provide personal and professional opportunities for young women to promote their voices in culture, politics, and the community. It provides a forum for today's young women to express their viewpoints, talents, and accomplishments to audiences during the telecast and to the public at large during the ensuing year. Almost all contestants have either received, or are in the process of earning either college or postgraduate degrees, and utilize Miss America scholarship grants to further their educations.

PERSONAL SHOPPER

Association of Image Consultants International (AICI)
431 East Locust Street, Suite 300
Des Moines, IA 50309
(515) 282-5500
info@aici.org
http://aici.org

There is no professional organization specifically for personal shoppers. But since many image consultants offer personal shopping services, personal shoppers may be interested in becoming members of the Association of Image Consultants International, a worldwide, nonprofit organization for individuals offering image consulting services. Among the goals of the AICI are enhancing the professionalism, credibility, and advancement of image consulting. They assist members in building their businesses; and they provide support, training, and networking opportunities through regional chapters and an annual convention. The AICI also offers certification. Members can earn the First Level of Certification (FLC), and then go on to become a Certified Image Professional (CIP), or a Certified Image Master (CIM). You can search their online directory and find an image consultant near you.

PIANO TECHNICIAN

Piano Technicians Guild, Inc.
4444 Forest Avenue
Kansas City, KS 66106-3750
(913) 432-9975
info@ptg.org
http://www.ptg.org

The PTG is a nonprofit organization for piano technicians. The missions of the PTG are to provide educational information and opportunities to piano technicians, and to offer certification to qualified PTG members. With no national requirements for licensing, PTG has established and maintains standards of workmanship in the area of piano repair. The PTG Web site contains an amazing amount of information related to pianos and piano repair. Containing links to information about local PTG chapters, RPT exams, training programs, piano images and history, mailing lists and newsgroups, and other music resources, the PTG home page is a great starting point for anyone interested in becoming a piano technician.

Piano Technicians Journal
4444 Forest Avenue
Kansas City, KS 66106-3750
(913) 432-9975
http://www.ptg.org/ptj/index.html
Published monthly, Piano Technicians Journal *is the official publication of the*

Piano Technicians Guild (PTG). Each issue contains articles written by experts in the field of piano technology. A subscription to the Journal is included with PTG membership, but stand-alone subscriptions are also available. Back issues are available. Issues from 1979 to 1999 are available on a set of searchable CDs.

PROFESSIONAL ORGANIZER

National Association of Professional Organizers (NAPO)
4700 West Lake Avenue
Glenview, IL 60025
(847) 375-4746
hq@napo.net
http://www.napo.net

Founded in 1985, the National Association of Professional Organizers (NAPO) is a nonprofit professional organization for individuals in the professional organizing trade or related areas, such as manufacturers of organizing products and supplies. With more than 3,350 members from the United States and eight foreign countries, it is the largest professional association of its kind in the world. There are more than 20 local NAPO chapters. The association works to develop and promote the profession and industry. They have worked to establish a code of ethics governing professional conduct throughout the organizing profession. NAPO offers educational materials and training opportunities. Members receive a bimonthly newsletter with the latest news and information in and about the organizing profession and industry.

Red Letter Day Professional Organizers
(586) 746-1428
Info@RLDPO.com
http://www.rldpo.com

Web site operated by professional organizer Debbie Stanley, with FAQs, resources, a newsletter, and lots of organizing information.

WATCH AND CLOCK REPAIRER

American Watchmakers-Clockmakers Institute (AWCI)

701 Enterprise Drive
Harrison, OH 45030-1696
(513) 367-9800
http://www.awci.com

The American Watchmakers-Clockmakers Institute (AWCI) is a not-for-profit professional trade association for persons working in and interested in preserving and promoting the standards of workmanship in horology worldwide. The beginnings of the AWCI date back to what is believed to be America's first watchmakers' society, founded in 1866 in New York City by German immigrant watchmakers. Today, the AWCI works to establish standards for the repair and restoration taught to watch and clock repairers around the world. The AWCI Web site maintains a list of schools of horology. To help members continue to grow and learn in their knowledge, they offer a wide range of continuing education courses at their Harrison, Ohio training center, bench courses that travel around the country, a home study course in clock repair, and the annual AWCI meeting. The AWCI offers six levels of certification in watch and clock making (and repair). The certification is earned by passing the appropriate proficiency exam. AWCI membership includes a subscription to Horological Times. *Inside each monthly issue, members will find articles about servicing timepieces, using shop tools and equipment, repair techniques, and much more.*

Clockmakers Newsletter
203 John Glenn Avenue
Reading, PA 19607

Published monthly, the eight-page Clockmakers Newsletter *is devoted to the repair and restorations of only clocks. Articles focus on practical repairs and include photos and drawings to illustrate the text. A searchable index and forum are available at the Web site. All back issues and a print index are also available to purchase.*

National Association of Watch and Clock Collectors, Inc. (NAWCC)

514 Poplar Street
Columbia, PA 17512
(717) 684-8261
http://www.nawcc.org

Founded in 1943, The National Association of Watch and Clock Collectors, Inc. (NAWCC) is a nonprofit organization made up of professionals, collectors, and other individuals interested in timepieces. The NAWCC offers a clock repair program, a watch repair program, and a complete horological repair program (both clock and watch repair) at a campus located at their headquarters in Lancaster County, Pennsylvania. The association's headquarters also houses the largest horological reference collection in the country. Members may borrow items from the library's collection. The National Watch & Clock Museum is also located at the Lancaster Country headquarters. NAWCC chapters around the country give collectors, hobbyists, repair professionals, and other members the chance to interact with one another and learn more about their shared interests. "Suitcase Workshops," regional conventions, symposiums, and an annual national convention give watch and clock repairers an opportunity to learn additional skills and techniques. NAWCC membership includes a subscription to the journal BULLETIN, *which features articles on various aspects of timekeeping and timekeeping pieces, as well as a variety of other information about NAWCC activities and more.*

WEDDING PLANNER

Association of Certified Professional Wedding Consultants
7791 Prestwick Circle
San Josse, CA 95135
(408) 528-9000
http://www.acpwc.com

The Association of Certified Professional Wedding Consultants (ACPWC) is the primary registered training and certification program for Wedding Consultants. ACPWC offers a five-day personalized training course, a three-day extended weekend class, seminars and a home study program for Wedding Planners/ Wedding Consultants and Church and Facility Coordinators. Graduate members of the Association of Certified Professional Wedding Consultants have the opportunity to achieve Professional status and Certification, and benefit from the continuing education support system offered by the association.

Association for Wedding Professionals
6700 Freeport Boulevard, Suite 202
Sacramento, CA 95822
(916) 392-5000

AFWPI is an international organization dedicated to providing quality service and a central source of information and referrals for those planning weddings and those who service weddings.

APPENDIX B. ONLINE CAREER RESOURCES

This volume offers a look inside a wide range of unusual and unique careers that might appeal to someone interested in jobs in the service sector. While it highlights general information, it's really only a glimpse into these jobs. The entries are intended to merely whet your appetite and provide you with some career options you may never have known existed.

Before jumping into any career, you'll want to do more research to make sure that it's really something you want to pursue. That way, as you continue to research and talk to people in those particular fields, you can ask informed and intelligent questions that will help you make your decisions. You might want to research the education options for learning the skills you'll need to be successful, along with scholarships, work-study programs, and other opportunities to help you finance that education. And you might want answers to questions that weren't addressed in the information provided here. If you search long enough, you can find just about anything using the Internet, including additional information about the jobs featured in this book.

✳ **A word about Internet safety:** The Internet is a wonderful resource for networking. Many job and career sites have forums where students can interact with other people interested in and working in that field. Some sites even offer online chats where people can communicate with each other in real time. They provide students and jobseekers opportunities to make connections and maybe even begin to lay the groundwork for future employment. But as you use these forums and chats remember, anyone could be on the other side of that computer screen, telling you exactly what you want to hear. It's easy to get wrapped up in the excitement of the moment when you're in a forum or a chat, interacting with people who share your career interests and aspirations. Be cautious about what kind of personal information you make available on the forums and in the chats; never give out your full name, address, or phone number. And never agree to meet with someone you've met online.

SEARCH ENGINES

When looking for information, there are lots of search engines that will help you to find out more about these jobs along with others that might interest you. While you might already have a favorite search engine, you might want to take some time to check out some of the others. Several engines will offer suggestions for ways to narrow your results, or related phrases you might want to search along with your search results. This is handy if you are having trouble locating exactly what you want.

It's also a good idea to learn how to use the advanced search features of your favorite search engines so you can zero in on exactly the information for which you're searching without wasting time looking through pages of irrelevant hits.

As you use the Internet to search for information on the perfect career, keep in mind that like anything you find on the Internet, you need to consider the source from which the information comes.

Some of the most popular Internet search engines are:

AllSearchEngines.com
www.allsearchengines.com

This search engine index has links to the major search engines along with search engines grouped by topic. The site includes a page with more than 75 career and job search engines at http://www. allsearchengines.com/careerjobs.html.

AlltheWeb
http://www.alltheweb.com

AltaVista
http://www.altavista.com

Ask.com
http://www.ask.com

Dogpile
http://www.dogpile.com

Excite
http://www.excite.com

Google
http://www.google.com

HotBot
http://www.hotbot.com

LookSmart
http://www.looksmart.com

Lycos
http://www.lycos.com

Mamma.com
http://www.mamma.com

MSN Network
http://www.msn.com

My Way
http://www.goto.com

Teoma
http://www.directhit.com

Vivisimo
http://www.vivisimo.com

Yahoo!
http://www.yahoo.com

HELPFUL WEB SITES

The Internet is a wealth of information on careers—everything from the mundane to the outrageous. There are thousands of sites devoted to helping you find the perfect job for you and your interests, skills, and talents. The sites listed here are some of the most helpful ones that the authors discovered while researching the jobs in this volume. The sites are listed in alphabetical order. They are offered for your information, and are not endorsed by the authors.

All Experts
http://www.allexperts.com

"The oldest & largest free Q&A service on the Internet," AllExperts.com has thousands of volunteer experts to answer your questions. You can also read replies to questions asked by other people. Each expert has an online profile to help you pick someone who might be best suited to answer your question. Very easy to use, it's a great resource for finding experts who can help to answer your questions.

America's Career InfoNet
http://www.acinet.org

A wealth of information. You can get a feel for the general job market; check out wages and trends in a particular state for different jobs; and learn more about the knowledge, skills, abilities, and tasks for specific careers; and learn about required certifications and how to get them. You

can search over 5,000 scholarship and
other financial opportunities to help you
further your education. A huge career
resources library has links to nearly
6,500 online resources. And for fun,
you can take a break and watch one of
nearly 450 videos featuring real people at
work; everything from custom tailors to
engravers, glassblowers to silversmiths.

Backdoor Jobs: Short-Term Job Adventures, Summer Jobs, Volunteer Vacations, Work Abroad and More
http://www.backdoorjobs.com

This is the Web site of the popular book
by the same name, now in its third
edition. While not as extensive as the
book, the site still offers a wealth of
information for people looking for short-
term opportunities: internships, seasonal
jobs, volunteer vacations, and work
abroad situations. Job opportunities
are classified into several categories:
Adventure Jobs, Camps, Ranches &
Resort Jobs, Ski Resort Jobs, Jobs in the
Great Outdoors, Nature Lover Jobs,
Sustainable Living and Farming Work,
Artistic & Learning Adventures, Heart
Work, and Opportunities Abroad.

Boston Works—Job Explainer
http://bostonworks.boston.com/globe/
job_explainer/archive.html

For nearly 18 months, the Boston
Globe ran a weekly series profiling
a wide range of careers. Some of the
jobs were more traditional, but with
a twist, such as the veterinarian who
makes house calls. Others were very
unique and unusual, like the profile of a
Superior of Society monk. The profiles
discuss an "average" day, challenges of
the job, required training, salary, and
more. Each profile gives an up close,
personal look at that particular career.
In addition, The Boston Works Web site

(http://bostonworks.boston.com) has a
lot of good, general employment-related
information.

Career Guide to Industries
http://www.bls.gov/oco/cg/cgindex.htm

For someone interested in working in a
specific industry, but maybe undecided
about exactly what career to pursue, this
site is the place to start. Put together by
the U.S. Department of Labor, you can
learn more about the industry, working
conditions, employment, occupations (in
the industry), training and advancement,
earnings, outlook, and sources of
additional information.

Career Planning at About.com
http://careerplanning.about.com

Like most of the other About.com
topics, the career planning area is a
wealth of information, and links to other
information on the Web. Among the
excellent essentials are career planning
A-to-Z, a career planning glossary,
information on career choices, and a
free career planning class. There are
many great articles and other excellent
resources.

Career Prospects in Virginia
http://www3.ccps.virginia.edu/career_
prospects/default-search.html

Career Prospects is a database of entries
with information about over 400 careers.
Developed by the Virginia Career
Resource Network, the online career
information resource of the Virginia
Department of Education, Office of
Career and Technical Education Services,
this site was intended as a source of
information about jobs "important to
Virginia" but it's actually a great source
of information for anyone. While some
of the information like wages, outlook,
and some of the requirements may apply

only to Virginia, the other information for each job, like what's it like, getting ahead, skills, and the links will be of help to anyone interested in that career.

Career Voyages
http://www.careervoyages.gov

"The ultimate road trip to career success," sponsored by the U.S. Department of Labor and the U.S. Department of Education. This site features sections for students, parents, career changers, and career advisors with information and resources aimed to that specific group. The FAQ offers great information about getting started, the high-growth industries, how to find your perfect job, how to make sure you're qualified for the job you want, tips for paying for the training and education you need, and more. Also interesting are the hot careers *and* the emerging fields.

Dream Jobs
http://www.salary.com/careers/
layouthtmls/crel_display_Cat10.html

The staff at Salary.com takes a look at some wild, wacky, outrageous, and totally cool ways to earn a living. The jobs they highlight include pro skateboarder, computer game guru, nose, diplomat, and much more. The profiles don't offer links or resources for more information, but they are informative and fun to read.

Find It! in DOL
http://www.dol.gov/dol/findit.htm

A handy source for finding information at the extensive U.S. Department of Labor Web site. You can "Find It!" by broad topic category, or by audience, which includes a section for students.

Fine Living: *Radical Sabbatical*
http://www.fineliving.com/fine/episode_
archive/0,1663,FINE_1413_14,00.
html#Series873

The show Radical Sabbatical *on the Fine Living network looks at people willing to take a chance and follow their dreams and passions. The show focuses on individuals between the ages of 20 and 65 who have made the decision to leave successful, lucrative careers to start over, usually in an unconventional career. You can read all about these people and their journeys on the show's Web site.*

Free Salary Survey Reports and Cost of Living Reports
http://www.salaryexpert.com

Based on information from a number of sources, Salary Expert will tell you what kind of salary you can expect to make for a certain job in a certain geographic location. Salary Expert has information on hundreds of jobs; everything from your more traditional white- and blue-collar jobs, to some unique and out of the ordinary professions like acupressurist, blacksmith, denture waxer, taxidermist, and many others. With sections covering schools, crime, community comparison, community explorer, and more, the moving center *is a useful area for people who need to relocate for training or employment.*

Fun Jobs
http://www.funjobs.com

Fun Jobs has job listings for adventure, outdoor, and fun jobs at ranches, camps, ski resorts, and more. The job postings have a lot of information about the position, requirements, benefits, and responsibilities so that you know what you are getting into ahead of time. And, you can apply online for most of the positions. The Fun Companies link *will let you look up companies in an A-to-Z listing, or you can search for companies in a specific area or by keyword. The company listings offer you more detailed information about the location, types of jobs available, employment qualifications, and more.*

Girls Can Do

http://www.girlscando.com

"Helping girls discover their life's passions," Girls Can Do has opportunities, resources, and a lot of other cool stuff for girls ages 8 to 18. Girls can explore sections on Outdoor Adventure, Sports, My Body, The Arts, Sci-Tech, Change the World, *and* Learn, Earn, and Intern. *In addition to reading about women in all sorts of careers, girls can explore a wide range of opportunities and information that will help them grow into strong, intelligent, capable women.*

Great Web Sites for Kids

http://www.ala.org/gwstemplate.cfm?section=greatwebsites&template=/cfapps/gws/default.cfm

Great Web Sites for Kids is a collection of more than 700 sites organized into a variety of categories, including animals, sciences, the arts, reference, social sciences, and more. All of the sites included here have been approved by a committee made up of professional librarians and educators. You can even submit your favorite site for possible inclusion.

Hospitality Jobs Online

http://www.hospitalityonline.com

Hospitality Jobs Online features worldwide resort jobs with ski and snowboard resorts, camps, national parks, cruise ships, restaurants and hotels. The site includes a newsletter, job profiles, articles and advice, and all sorts of job ads.

Hot Jobs: Career Tools Home

http://www.hotjobs.com/htdocs/tools/index-us.html

While the jobs listed at Hot Jobs are more on the traditional side, the Career Tools *area has a lot of great resources for anyone looking for a job. You'll find information about how to write a resume and a cover letter, how to put together a career portfolio, interviewing tips, links to career assessments, and much more.*

Job Descriptions & Job Details

http://www.job-descriptions.org

Search for descriptions and details for more than 13,000 jobs at this site. You can search for jobs by category or by industry. You'd probably be hard pressed to find a job that isn't listed here, and you'll probably find lots of jobs you never imagined existed. The descriptions and details are short, but it's interesting and fun, and might lead you to the career of your dreams.

Job Hunter's Bible

http://www.jobhuntersbible.com

This site is the official online supplement to the book What Color Is Your Parachute? A Practical Manual for Job-Hunters and Career-Changers, *and is a great source of information with lots of informative, helpful articles and links to many more resources.*

Job Profiles

http://www.jobprofiles.org

A collection of profiles, where, "Experienced Workers Share: Rewards of their job; Stressful parts of the job; Basic skills the job demands; Challenges of the future; and, Advice on entering the field." The careers include everything from baseball ticket manager to pastry chef and much, much more. The hundreds of profiles are arranged by broad category. While most of the profiles are easy to read, you can checkout the How to browse JobProfileS. org *section (http://www.jobprofiles.org/jphowto.htm) if you have any problems.*

Major Job Web sites at Careers.org

http://www.careers.org/topic/01_jobs_10.html

This page at the careers.org Web site has links for more than 40 of the Web's major job-related Web sites. While you're there, check out the numerous links to additional information.

Monster Jobs

http://www.monster.com

Monster.com is one of the largest, and probably best known, job resource sites on the Web. It's really one-stop shopping for almost anything job-related that you can imagine. You can find a new job, network, update your resume, improve your skills, plan a job change or relocation, and so much more. Of special interest are the Monster: Cool Careers (http://change. monster.com/archives/coolcareers) and the Monster: Job Profiles (http://jobprofiles. monster.com) where you can read about some really neat careers. The short profiles also include links to additional information. The Monster: Career Advice section (http://content.monster.com/) has resume and interviewing advice, message boards where you can network, relocation tools and advice, and more.

Occupational Outlook Handbook

http://www.bls.gov/oco

Published by the U.S. Department of Labor's Bureau of Labor Statistics, the Occupational Outlook Handbook *(sometimes referred to as the* OOH) *is the premiere source of career information. The book is updated every two years, so you can be assured that the information you are using to help make your decisions is current. The online version is very easy to use; you can search for a specific occupation, browse though a group of related occupations, or look through an alphabetical listing of all the jobs included*

in the volume. Each of the entries will highlight the general nature of the job, working conditions, training and other qualifications, job outlook, average earning, related occupations, and sources of additional information. Each entry covers several pages and is a terrific source to get some great information about a huge variety of jobs.

ResortJobs.com

http://www.resortjobs.com

ResortJobs.com features worldwide resort jobs with ski and snowboard resorts, camps, national parks, cruise ships, restaurants, and hotels. The site includes a newsletter, job profiles, articles and advice, and all sorts of job ads.

The Riley Guide: Employment Opportunities and Job Resources on the Internet

http://www.rileyguide.com

The Riley Guide is an amazing collection of job and career resources. Unless you are looking for something specific, one of the best ways to maneuver around the site is with the A-to-Z index. You can find everything from links to careers in enology to information about researching companies and employers. The Riley Guide is a great place to find just about anything you might be looking for, and probably lots of things you aren't looking for. But, be forewarned, it's easy to get lost in the A-Z Index, reading about all sorts of interesting things.

USA TODAY Career Focus

http://www.usatoday.com/careers/dream/dreamarc.htm

Several years ago, USA TODAY *ran a series featuring people working in their dream jobs. In the profiles, people discuss how they got their dream job, what they enjoy the most about it, they talk about an average day, their education backgrounds, sacrifices they had to make for their jobs, and more. They also share words of advice for anyone hoping to follow in their footsteps. Most of the articles also feature links where you can find more information. The USATODAY. Com Job Center (http://www.usatoday. com/money/jobcenter/front.htm) also has links to lots of resources and additional information.*

CAREER TESTS AND INVENTORIES

If you have no idea what career is right for you, there are many resources available online that will help assess your interests and maybe steer you in the right direction. While some of the assessments charge a fee, there are many out there that are free. You can locate more tests and inventories by doing an Internet search for "career tests," "career inventories," or "personality inventories." Some of the most popular assessments available online are:

Campbell Interest and Skill Survey (CISS)
http://www.usnews.com/usnews/edu/careers/ccciss.htm

Career Explorer
http://careerexplorer.net/aptitude.asp

Career Focus 2000 Interest Inventory
http://www.iccweb.com/careerfocus

The Career Key
http://www.careerkey.org

CAREERLINK Inventory
http://www.mpc.edu/cl/cl.htm

Career Maze
http://www.careermaze.com/home.asp?licensee=CareerMaze

Career Tests at CareerPlanner.com
http://www.careerplanner.com

FOCUS
http://www.focuscareer.com

Keirsey Temperament Test
http://www.keirsey.com

Motivational Appraisal of Personal Potential (MAPP)
http://www.assessment.com

Myers-Briggs Personality Type
http://www.personalitypathways.com/type_inventory.html

Princeton Review Career Quiz
http://www.princetonreview.com/cte/quiz/default.asp

Skills Profiler
http://www.acinet.org/acinet/skills_home.asp

READ MORE ABOUT IT

AAA HOTEL RATER

Rutes, Walter A., Richard H. Penner, and Lawrence Adams. *Hotel Design, Planning, and Development*. New York: W.H. Norton & Company, 2001.

Rutherford, Denney G. *Hotel Management and Operations*. New York: Wiley, 2001.

AMERICAN SIGN LANGUAGE INTERPRETER

Lazorisak, Carole, and Dawn Donohue. *Complete Idiot's Guide to Conversational Sign Language Illustrated*. New York: Alpha Books, 2004.

Stewart, David. *American Sign Language the Easy Way*. New York: Barron's Educational Series, 1995.

AQUARIUM MAINTENANCE SERVICE PROVIDER

Boruchowitz, David E. *The Simple Guide to Fresh Water Aquariums*. Neptune City, N.J.: TFH Publications, 2001.

Burkhart, Alice, Richard Crow, and Dave Keeley. *Pocket Guide to the Care and Maintenance of Aquarium Fish*. London: PRC, 2002.

Dakin, Nick. *Complete Encyclopedia of the Saltwater Aquarium*. Toronto: Firefly Books, 2003.

Dawes, John. *Complete Encyclopedia of the Freshwater Aquarium*. Willowdale, Ont.: Firefly Books, 2001.

Hiscock, Peter. *Encyclopedia of Aquarium Plants*. Hauppage, N.Y.: Barron's, 2003.

Michael, Scott W. *Marine Fishes: 500+ Essential-To-Know Aquarium Species*

(The Pocketexpert Guide Series for Aquarists and Underwater Naturalists, 1). Neptune City, N.J.: TFH Publications, 1999.

Paletta, Michael S. *The New Marine Aquarium: Step-By-Step Setup & Stocking Guide*. Neptune City, N.J.: TFH Publications, 1999.

Scott, Peter W. *Complete Aquarium*. New York: DK, 1995.

BEER TAP CLEANER

Swierczynski, Duane. *The Big Book o' Beer: Everything You Ever Wanted to Know About the Greatest Beverage on Earth*. Philadelphia: Quirk Books, 2004.

BIKE MESSENGER

Culley, Travis. *The Immortal Class : Bike Messengers and the Cult of Human Power*. New York: Random House, 2002.

Hurst, Robert. *The Art of Urban Cycling : Lessons from the Street*. Guilford, Conn. Falcon, 2004.

BODY PARTS MODEL

Esch, Natasha and C.I. Walker. *Wilhelmina Guide to Modeling*. New York: Fireside, 1996.

Roshumba. *The Complete Idiot's Guide to Being a Model*. New York: Alpha Books, 2001.

BRAILLE TRANSCRIBER

Dorf, Maxine. *Instruction Manual for Braille Transcribing: Supplement: Drills Reproduced in Braille*. Louisville, Ky.:

American Printing House for the Blind, 1976.

Burns, Mary F. *The Burns Braille Transcription Dictionary*. Louisville, Ky.: American Printing House for the Blind, 1991.

BROADCAST CAPTIONER

Daniel, Kevin. *Writing Naked: Principles of Writing for Realtime and Captioning*. Vienna, Va.: National Court Reporters Association, 1988.

Robson, Gary D. *The Closed Captioning Handbook*. Burlington, Mass.: Focal Press, 2004.

BUTLER

Allen, Kimberly. *A Butler's Life: Scenes from the Other Side of the Silver Salver*. IUniverse.com: Authors Choice Press, 2001.

Ferry, Steven. *Butlers & Household Managers: 21st Century Professionals*. North Charleston, S.C.: Words & Images, 2002.

Radke, Linda F. *Household Careers: Nannies, Butlers, Maids & More: The Complete Guide for Finding Household Employment or "If the Dog Likes You, You're Hired!"* Chandler, Ariz.: 5 Star Publications, 1993.

Roberts, Robert. *Roberts' Guide for Butlers and Household Staff*. Bedford, Mass.: Applewood Books, 1988.

CAREER COUNSELOR

Bolles, Richard Nelson, and Mark Bolles. *What Color Is Your Parachute 2006: A Practical Manual for Jobhunters And Career*. Berkeley, Calif.: Ten Speed Press, 2005.

Figler, Howard E., and Richard N. Bolles. *The Career Counselor's Handbook*. Berkeley, Calif.: Ten Speed Press, 1999.

Lore, Nicholas. *The Pathfinder: How to Choose or Change Your Career for a Lifetime of Satisfaction and Success*. New York: Simon & Schuster, 1998.

Tieger, Paul D., and Barbara Barron-Tieger. *Do What You Are: Discover the Perfect Career for You Through the Secrets of Personality Type—Revised and Updated Edition Featuring E-careers for the 21st Century, 3rd ed.* Boston : Little, Brown, 2001.

ETIQUETTE CONSULTANT

Biech, Elaine. *The Consultant's Quick Start Guide: An Action Plan for Your First Year in Business*. San Francisco: Pfeiffer, 2001.

Dresser, Norine. *Multicultural Manners : Essential Rules of Etiquette for the 21st Century*. New York: John Wiley & Sons, 2005.

FITTING MODEL

Esch, Natasha, and C.I. Walker. *Wilhelmina Guide to Modeling*. New York: Fireside, 1996.

Roshumba. *The Complete Idiot's Guide to Being a Model*. New York: Alpha Books, 2001.

FORTUNE COOKIE WRITER

Read, Margery. *The Fortune Cookie Book*. Nashville: Cumberland House Publishing, 1997.

FUNERAL DIRECTOR

Howarth, Glennys. *Last Rites: The Work of the Modern Funeral Director (Death, Value and Meaning)*. Amityville, N.Y.: Baywood Publishing Company, Inc., 1996.

Sacks, Terence J. *Opportunities in Funeral Services Careers*. Lincolnwood, Ill.: VGM Career Books, 1997.

FUNERAL HOME COSMETOLOGIST

Sacks, Terence J. *Opportunities in Funeral Services Careers.* Lincolnwood, Ill.: VGM Career Books, 1997.

GOVERNESS

Radke, Linda F. *Household Careers: Nannies, Butlers, Maids & More: The Complete Guide for Finding Household Employment or "If the Dog Likes You, You're Hired! "*Chandler, Ariz.: 5 Star Publications, 1993.

HOLIDAY DECORATOR

Cole, Peter, Frankie Frankeny, and Leslie Jonath. *Christmas Trees: Fun and Festive Ideas.* San Francisco: Chronicle Books, 2002.

Finkle, Brad. *Holiday Hero: A Step-By-Step Guide to Decorating Your Home's Exterior and Yard for the Holidays.* Omaha, Nebr.: Creative Decorating, 2003.

Patoski, Christina. *Merry Christmas, America: A Front Yard View of the Holidays.* Charlottesville, Va.: Thomasson-Grant, 1994.

Sanna, Ellyn. *101 Tree Trimming Ideas (Homemade Christmas).* Uhrichsville, Ohio: Barbour, 2003.

Seidman, David. *Holiday Lights!: Brilliant Displays to Inspire Your Christmas Celebration.* North Adams, Mass.: Storey, 2003.

Staron, Debi, and Bob Pranga. *Christmas Style.* New York: DK, 2004.

HOME STAGER

Fisher, Jeanette J. *Sell Your Home for Top Dollar—FAST! Design Psychology for Redesign and Home Staging.* Lake Elsinore, Calif.: Family Trust, 2005.

Matzke, Lori. *Home Staging: Creating Buyer-Friendly Rooms to Sell Your House.* Arlington, Minn.: Center Stage Home, 2004.

Schwarz, Barb. *Home Staging: The Winning Way to Sell Your House for More Money.* New York: Wiley, 2006.

HOTEL CONCIERGE

Giovanni, K.C., and Ron Giovanni. *The Concierge Manual.* Apex, N.C.: New Road Publishing, 2002.

Stiel, Holly, and Delta Collins. *Ultimate Service: The Complete Handbook to the World of the Concierge.* Upper Saddle River, N.J.: Prentice Hall, 1994.

INNSITTER

Riggs, R.J. *Innsights: An Innsitter's Tale.* Frederick, Md.: PublishAmerica, 2004.

Craig, Susannah, and Park Davis. *Complete Idiot's Guide to Running a Bed and Breakfast.* New York: Alpha, 2001.

Brown, Susan, Pat Hardy, Jo Ann M. Bell, and Mary E. Davies. *So, You Want to Be An Innkeeper.* San Francisco: Chronicle Books, 2004.

LOCKSMITH

Phillips, Bill. *Locksmithing, 3rd ed.* New York: McGraw Hill, 1999.

———. *Professional Locksmithing Techniques, 2nd ed.* New York: TAB Books, 1996.

———. *The Complete Book of Locks and Locksmithing, 6th ed.* New York: McGraw-Hill, 2005.

Rathjen, Joseph E. *Locksmithing: From Apprentice to Master.* New York: McGraw-Hill, 1995.

MATCHMAKER

Clampitt, Lisa, Jerome Chasques, and Blaise C. Hancock, edited by Tracy Rohrer, Blaise C. Hancock. *Matchmaking from Fun to Profit: The Matchmaking Institute's Guide to Becoming a Matchmaker.* New York: Matchmaking Institute, Inc., 2006.

MYSTERY SHOPPER

Gow, Kailin. *How to Have Fun and Make Money in Mystery Shopping: A How-To Workbook with Leads to Get Started Right Away!* Irving, Tex.: Sparklesoup Studios, 2002.

Newhouse, Ilisha S. *Mystery Shopping Made Simple.* New York: McGraw-Hill, 2004.

Obarski, Anne M. *Surprising Secrets of Mystery Shoppers: 10 Steps to Quality Service That Keep Customers Coming Back!* Tarentum, Ark.: Word Association Publishers, 2003.

Poynter, James M. *Mystery Shopping: Get Paid to Shop, 4th ed.* Denver, Colo.: Leromi, 2002.

Stucker, Cathy. *The Mystery Shopper's Manual, 6th ed.* Sugar Land, Tex.: Special Interests Publishing, 2004.

Weis, Julie, and Lynette Janec. *How to Start and Run Your Own Mystery Shopping Company.* Aventura, Fla.: Basic Success, 2000.

NANNY

Radke, Linda F. *Household Careers: Nannies, Butlers, Maids & More: The Complete Guide for Finding Household Employment or "If the Dog Likes You, You're Hired!"* Chandler, Ariz.: 5 Star Publications, 1993.

Carlton, Susan, and Coco Myers. *The Nanny Book: The Smart Parent's Guide to Hiring, Firing, and Every Sticky Situation in Between.* New York: St. Martin's Griffin, 1999.

Bassett, Monica M. *The Professional Nanny.* New York: Thomson Delmar Learning, 1997.

PAGEANT CONSULTANT

Bordenkircher, S.A. *How to Win Your Crown: A Teen's Guide to Pageant Competition.* Camaeron, W.Va.: Abby Publishing, 1998.

Goulet, Tag, and Rachel Gurevich. *FabJob Guide to Become an Image Consultant.* Seattle: FabJob.com Ltd., 2005.

Nix-Rice, Nancy, and Pati Palmer. *Looking Good: A Comprehensive Guide to Wardrobe Planning, Color & Personal Style Development.* Portland, Ore.: Palmer/Pletsch Publishing, 1996.

PERSONAL SHOPPER

Lumpkin, Emily S. *Get Paid to Shop: Be a Personal Shopper for Corporate America, 1st ed.* Columbia, S.C.: Forté, 1999.

Marks, Lynne Henderson, and Dominique Isbecque. *The Perfect Fit: How to Start an Image Consulting Business.* Orlando, Fla.: FirstPublish, Inc., 2001.

York-McDaniel, Brenda. *Image Consulting for the 21st Century.* Peoria, Ariz.: Academy of Fashion & Image, 2000.

PIANO TECHNICIAN

Fischer, J. Cree. *Piano Tuning: A Simple and Accurate Method for Amateurs.* New York: Dover, 1975.

Booth, George W. *Pianos, Piano Tuners and Their Problems.* London: Janus, 1996.

Reblitz, Arthur A. *Piano Servicing, Tuning, and Rebuilding for the Professional, the Student, and the Hobbyist, 2nd ed.* Vestal, N.Y.: Vestal, 1993.

PROFESSIONAL ORGANIZER

Glovinsky, Cindy. *Making Peace with the Things in Your Life: Why Your Papers, Books, Clothes, and Other Possessions Keep Overwhelming You and What to Do About It, 1st ed.* New York: St. Martin's Griffin, 2002.

Kolberg, Judith, and Kathleen Nadeau. *ADD-Friendly Ways to Organize Your Life.* New York: Brunner-Routledge, 2002.

Morgenstern, Julie. *Organizing from the Inside Out: The Foolproof System for Organizing Your Home, Your Office and Your Life, 2nd ed.* New York: Henry Holt, 2004.

Smallin, Donna. *Organizing Plain and Simple: A Ready Reference Guide with Hundreds of Solutions to Your Everyday Clutter Challenges.* North Adams, Mass.: Storey Books, 2002.

Stanley, Debbie. *Organize Your Home In No Time.* Indianapolis, Ind.: Que, 2005.

———. *Organize Your Personal Finances In No Time.* Indianapolis, Ind.: Que, 2005.

Starr, Meryl. *Home Organizing Workbook: Clearing Your Clutter, Step by Step.* San Francisco: Chronicle Books, 2004.

Waddill, Kathy. *The Organizing Sourcebook: Nine Strategies for Simplifying Your Life.* Chicago: Contemporary Books, 2001.

Walsh, Peter. *How to Organize (Just About) Everything: More Than 500 Step-by-Step Instructions for Everything from Organizing Your Closets to Planning a Wedding to Creating a Flawless Filing System.* New York: Free Press, 2004.

WATCH AND CLOCK REPAIRER

Balcomb, Philip E. *The Clock Repair Primer: The Beginner's Handbook: A Beginner's Introduction to the Mechanics of Pendulum Clocks and Basic Clock Repair.* Tell City, Ind.: Tempus, 1986.

Conover, Steven G. *Clock Repair: Basics.* Reading, Pa.: Clockmakers Newsletter, 1996.

De Carle, Donald. *Practical Watch Repairing.* London: NAG, 1992.

Fried, Henry B. *Bench Practices for Watch and Clockmakers.* New York: Columbia Communications, 1974.

Gazeley, W. J. *Clock and Watch Escapements.* New York: Van Nostrand Reinhold, 1982.

Harris, H. G. *Advanced Watch and Clock Repair.* Buchanan, N.Y.: Emerson Books, 1973.

Kelly, Harold C. *Clock Repairing As a Hobby.* New York: Association Press, 1972.

Penman, Laurie. *The Clock Repairer's Handbook.* Newton Abbot, Devon, United Kingdom: David & Charles; New York: Arco, 1985.

Whiten, A. J. *Repairing Old Clocks and Watches.* London: NAG, 1982.

WEDDING PLANNER

Ambarian, Sara L. *Bride's Touch: A Handbook of Wedding Personality and Inspiration.* Gresham, Ore.: Symbios, 1997.

Moran, Jill. *How to Start a Home-Based Event Planning Business.* Guilford, Conn.: Globe Pequot, 2004.

Phillips, Cho, and Sherrie Wilkolaski. *How To Start A Wedding Planning Business.* The Wedding Planning Institute, 2003.

Sandlin, Eileen Figure. *Start Your Own Wedding Consultant Business: Your Step-By-Step Guide to Success.* New York: Entrepreneur Press, 2003.

INDEX